DRAMA AND THE SEARCH FOR Mr./ Ms. RIGHT:

Understanding the cycle of mistreatment

By Raymond C. Adamore

African American IMAGES

Chicago, Illinois

Front cover illustration by Damon Stanford

First Edition, First Printing

Printed in the United States of America

10-DIGIT ISBN #: 0-910030-18-9

13-DIGIT ISBN #: 978-0910030-182

Dedication

To the women who made this book possible, BRENDA, "MY ANGEL," and TANIA.

Contents

Acknowledgments   v i

Introduction   v i i

Chapter 1: History of the African-American   1

      Ancestry   1

      American Slavery   4

Chapter 2: Prelude to the Mating Game   9

      Marriage Training   9

      The Search   12

Chapter 3: The Mating Game   21

      Protocols of the Mating Game   21

      Mating Game - Phase I   22

      Mating Game - Phase II   36

Chapter 4: The Decisions   51

      Living Together   51

      The Marriage Decision   56

Chapter 5: When Love is not Enough   59

     Wants and Needs   59

     The Aftermath   60

     The Language of Conflict   62

     The Role of Anger   66

     The Introduction of Violence   69

Chapter 6: New Directions   75

     African Threads   76

     Myths and Illusions   77

     The Language of Cooperation   79

     Reduction of Violence   85

     Counseling Assistance   89

Appendix A   92

     Adamore's Relationship Questionnaire   92

Appendix B   108

     Methodology   108

Appendix C   110

     Demographic Information   110

References   113

Acknowledgments

Since most human endeavors are not accomplished alone, this is also true of this effort. Therefore, I would like to thank those whose efforts have helped me to complete this book. First, I would like to give a special thanks to Dr. Rachel Lindsey, Dean, College of Arts & Sciences, Chicago State University (CSU), for her support, the various CSU faculty members that gave me their permission to enter their classrooms and the CSU students who completed the Adamore Relationship Questionnaire (ARQ).

A special thanks goes to Drs. Bobbie Anthony and Tadesse W. Giorgis, Professors of Psychology, and Dr. Doris Perry, Professor of Sociology and Social Work, CSU, for their time and comments.

I would like to thank Olivia Harvell for her time and hard work in the development and administration of the ARQ.

I would also like to thank Corrine Compton, Barbara Thomas, Angie Tero, Gene Williams, Jim Bradshaw, Cherie and Bob Dupuis, Yvonne Jefferies, Arthur Amaker and Tanya Lloyd for their editing assistance and support.

I would like to thank Sandra Ragan, Director, Office of Human Resources, CSU, for her support and also, Troy Davenport and Tanya Lloyd for their support and computer assistance.

There is also a special thanks to Jerry Pittman of Kemetian Motif Computer Graphics, Chicago, Illinois, for his great graphic artwork.

And finally, to Ben Watende Mtundu (Ben Hupp), Jerry Medol, Brenda Flemming, Alfred Adamore and all those unnamed souls, who through conversation, argument and debate, dropped me a pearl of wisdom or forced me to reexamine my position.

Introduction

It seems that the issue of violence in intimate relationships, is centered on women as the "victim", men as the "perpetrator" and legal and additional punishment of the men for the medical aftermath. With the focus of violence being placed on the beatings; men have been portrayed as (1) having no feelings, (2) innately violent and (3) controlling. I do not feel that this portrayal of violence in intimate relationships does anything towards solving its causation or minimizing its occurrence.

There were two events that focused my attention on violence in intimate relationships. The first event was the killing of a female coworker, by her husband, during a marital break-up. This caused me to return to the college classroom, in an effort to learn more about human behavior.

In a continuation of this effort, I opened a mating/marital counseling service to gain some practical knowledge of the psychological/behavioral tendencies of couples in intimate relationships. About two years after I had opened my counseling service, the second event happened. I met Ben Watende Mtundu (Ben Hupp) who introduced me to Jerry Medol, group leader of the Kansas City Men's Group (KCMG). Mr. Medol introduced me to a conceptual framework for anger and its application to men's issues and behaviors. I continued to attend KCMG's quarterly meetings for about four years and eventually broaden the conceptual framework for anger to include the issues and behaviors of both men and women.

I spent twenty years counseling mating/marital couples and five of those years counseling men charged with domestic violence. In addition, I used my conceptual framework of anger in therapy with couples and with men charged with domestic violence. With the vast majority of my clientele being African-Americans, they became my focus group for this project.

Drama and the Search for Mr./Mrs. Right:
Understanding the Cycle of Mistreatment

In order to have a common basis for discussion and improvement in intimate relationships, I created the *Adamore's Relationship Questionnaire (ARQ)*. It was administered to 240 men and women, ranging in age from twenty-two to forty-three. The ARQ questions with their accompanying data were incorporated into the text and became the framework for this book.

Chapters 1 through 4, identifies the historical, sociological, and psychological causal precursors to violence in intimate relationships. It seems that the seeds for violence in African-American intimate relationships, can be traced to (1) the disconnect of African-Americans from their African culture and (2) their mind set as they go through the mating/marital process.

This disconnect between African-Americans and their African culture, is hardly talked about when there are discussions about African-American intimate relationships, however, it is the 300-pound gorilla in the room. It is part of the collective unconsciousness of African-Americans in discussions concerning family, economics, racism, politics, religion, intelligence and culture.

The problem with the mind set of most African-American couples, which I feel is common for most intimate couples, is the inclusion of their unresolved wants/needs (*mainly wants*); that was not addressed during the mating process, being brought into the marital relationship where they become the seeds for turmoil and divorce.

Chapters 5 and 6, deals with identifying the psychological/ behavioral precursors to violence in intimate relationships and how to minimize its occurrence. Because the "victim and perpetrator" are usually the only persons present at the time of a violent incident, an educational understanding of the *genesis of conflict* and couples counseling is presented as a more effective way to minimize the incidence of violence in intimate relationships.

A copy of the ARQ, the research methodology and demographic information on the sample group can be found in Appendix A, B and C.

I feel that there are some lessons to be learned by couples from this research, especially the material on conflict in Chapters Five and Six. Also throughout this book, I have included my comments where I deemed it necessary, to place the data in a context of reality.

There are many books on improving intimate relationships that do not seem to address the concerns of couples that have already determined that they were meant for each other and are trying to make the relationship work. Most of the books seem to be geared toward improving the individual and not the couple. The intent of this book is to help present and/or future couples, minimize violence in their mating/marital relationships.

Chapter 1

History of the African-American

In an effort to look at violence in African-American intimate relationships, we need to understand our African heritage. *If you do not know where you have been, you do not know where you are going.* In order to gain a historic perspective on violence in African-American intimate relationships, (1) we need to understand who we were prior to the Western European invasion of the African continent and (2) to acknowledge our time in slavery and its aftermath on the African-American family.

Ancestry
In an effort to gain that historic perspective, we need to look beyond the shores of America. We need to understand that Africa is a continent and not a country. Black is neither an ethnic group nor a culture. Africa is full of many different groups of people: some known (Egyptians, Moroccans and Ethiopians) and some not as well known (Akan, Bantu and Zulu). It is the birthplace of humankind and the homeland of our ancestors. Although we may not know where in Africa our ancestors were taken, we can at least claim the continent of Africa. By claiming the continent of Africa, we can claim a relationship to the (1) architects of the Pyramids, (2) the establishment of the first written language (Egyptian hieroglyphics), (3) the establishment of the first monotheistic religion (Aton) and (4) a claim to the sciences of Astrology (a precursor to Astronomy), Mathematics, and Anatomy.

Even though Africa may have many different groups of people, there seems to be a general consensus of opinion that Africans (1) have an extended family structure, (2) they honor

1

their dead family members (ancestors), (3) had a polytheistic religious orientation, (4) that they have an arranged marital system, and (5) engages in *polygamy.* And according to Ani Dike Egwuonwu, in *Marriage Problems in Africa,* the arranged marital custom consists of (1) the marriage decision, (2) parental approval and (3) the bride-price.

In *Implications for Effective Psychotherapy with African-American Families and Individuals,* author Jay Thomas Willis, gives an overview of African families: (1) that the African family was the basis of economic, political and social organization, (2) the family was more important than its individual members, (3) everyone in the family was respected and it was a sacrilege to disrespect the mother, (4) children cared for their old-age parents, (5) that women were not considered to be unequal or second-class, (6) the head of the African family was either the eldest male or the biological father, (7) the family blood line was traced through the mother and (8) the care of the children was the responsibility of the parents and community.

In traditional Africans societies, the parents or extended family members, teach the children (male and female) their marital roles before they reached the age of puberty.

An *arranged marriage* begins when an African man *decides that he wants to marry* a woman that he has been observing. He will inform his parents and they will find out as much information about the woman's family as they can. If the family proves to be acceptable, his parents will talk to her family. If there is an agreement between the two families *(parental approval)*; the man is allowed to approach the woman's family, for their permission to marry their daughter. The man will then be told the *bride-price,* which can be anything from a cow to thousands of dollars, that he will have to pay to her family to legitimize and stabilize the marriage and show that he is capable of

2

taking good care of a wife. The wedding will not take place until the bride-price has been paid. If there is any courtship, it will take place between the time of the payment of the bride-price and the wedding. However, sex and love mostly takes place after marriage instead of before.

Once the wedding has taken place, the couple will move into the man's house. It is expected that there will immediately be children to insure the continuation of the family line and kinship group. In some African societies, a large number of children are a sign of wealth.

If there are any problems within the marriage, the wife is sent back to her family for further instructions. If the wife does not return, a state of divorce will exist. If the ex-wife remarries, the new husband would have to reimburse the ex-husband his bride-price payment.

In traditional African cultures, the practice of *polygamy* seems to be an extension of the arranged marriage and is a legal marital system with specific guidelines. It seems that the purpose of polygamy was designed to provide financial support for the unattached woman. It is often the first wife that urges the husband to seek another wife as her companion and helper with her household duties. Sometimes, the first wife will choose the woman he will marry. The husband is required to provide for each wife in the same manner. With no traditional religious limit to the number of wives and with a bride-price to be paid for each wife; having many wives was seen as a sign of wealth.

Islam, which is now a major religion on the African continent, permits polygamy. In the Islamic religion, a man is allowed to have up to four wives. Polygamy is allowed in an effort to deal with the surplus of women and the sexual nature of mankind. In *Slavery: The African American Psychic Trauma,* co-authors Sultan A. Latif and Naimah Latif stated that these additional wives

3

must be women with children whose husband has been killed in war. In addition, the new husbands must be men who are financially able to support more than one wife. As regards Christian marriages, there is insistence on having only one wife.

Before the invasion of the African continent by the Western Europeans, the African family had been thriving, healthy and functioning for centuries.

American Slavery

With the invasion of the African continent by the Western Europeans, millions of Africans were taken in bondage to the mines and cotton, coffee and sugar cane fields of the Americas and the Caribbean, to be sold as unpaid laborers (slaves). *Africans are the only ethnic group where the vast majority of its members were brought to America against their will.*

During slave trafficking in America (1619-1808), of the Africans that reached the shores of the United States, the slave owners made a deliberate and systematic effort to demean and demoralize the Africans. Latif & Latif, in *Slavery: The African American Psychic Trauma,* stated that this was done by (1) cutting off hair and removing clothing so that there would be no sense of identity and/or status, (2) they separated groups that spoke the same language so that they could not organize an uprising, (3) created fear of the slave owner by brutally beating, mutilating and shackling any slave (male/female) for any infraction of the rules and doing this in the presence of other slaves, and (4) using rape as a tool to control the slaves.

Slaves and their offspring were the property of the slave owner to do with as he pleased (keep or sale) and if sold, never to be seen again. The slave owner would have sex with any slave woman that he owned. If there was a bond between the slave woman and a slave man, if the male slave would try to interfere, the slave owner would threaten the African woman with the selling of her man or her offspring. In this way the slave owner used the African woman to control the African man. Therefore, the slave owner would take control of the African woman and children from the African man. This resulted in the emasculation of the African man by creating an atmosphere where he was powerless to protect his wive(s), children or himself. The continued emasculation of the African-American man by the majority culture, can be felt to this present day.

The idea of a powerless African man was ingrained upon the conscious and unconscious mind of the African women and has been passed from generation to generation, through their collective unconsciousness, to their American descendants, until this day.

In 1808, when slave trafficking ended in the United States, in order for the slave owners to maintain a supply of slaves, they took up the practice of *slave breeding*. African women were forced to have sex with any slave or white man and the slave owners would keep any offspring.

According to Latif & Latif, in *Slavery: The African American Psychic Trauma,* American slavery destroyed the African man and woman's sense of permanency in marriage and removed the need for training offspring for marriage. It resulted in the African women developing a feeling of low self-worth and low self-esteem because they did not have control over their bodies. It also destroyed the moral values between Africa men and women.

When the Emancipation Proclamation became effective on January 1, 1863, the Africans that were still in slavery, had no means of viable support but to stay where they were and continue to work in the mines and fields at "slave wages." As they tried to reestablish their family bonding, they reclaimed the extended family structure. This was appropriate for the number of hands that it took to support the surviving African family descendants (African-Americans), still working in the mines and fields for slave wages. After the end of American slavery, for the social, economic and political separation of the races in the South, there was a continued *overt* racial onslaught upon the families of African-Americans, through Reconstruction and Jim Crow segregation. Between 1910 and 1930, The First Great Northern Migration of about 1.6 million African-Americans began to move to the Northern cities of New York, Chicago, Cleveland and Detroit, to partake in the higher paying jobs of the Industrial Revolution. What they found was racial, housing and economic discrimination. Because of the discrimination found and the move from an agricultural environment to an industrial environment, the African-American family began to resemble the two-parent family structure.

Between 1940 and 1960, The Second Great Migration of about five million African-Americans began to move out of the South to California and the Western States. In the South, the extended family structure was still in effect and in parts of the Northern cities, the two-parent family structure began to grow, however, with the continued overt racism and discrimination, the African-American family began to falter. In the 1960's, the American government's welfare program, Aid to Families with Dependent Children (AFDC), required mothers on AFDC not to have a man (husband or not, if "able-bodied"), living in the home. This rule was enforced by late night visits by welfare workers and in many cases, forced the African-American father to leave the family for their survival.

Also during this time, the social changes that were going on in America (1) the introduction of the birth control pill, (2) the Supreme Court's decision on abortion, (3) the Sexual Revolution and (4) the Women's Liberation Movement, helped influence the

6

development of the single-parent African-American family structure.

Since the 1970's, in the aftermath of the Civil Rights Movement and Integration, racism has taken a *covert* turn with regard to the African-American family. This is reflected in the fact that African-Americans have limited control over their economic development which keeps their formation of a stable family structure in constant peril. One reason for the subjective racism and discrimination against African-Americans is our skin color. Because of the biological reality of our skin color, it limits our ability to blend in with the majority of lighter-skinned ethnic groups within America. By being the last hired and the first fired, it has kept the African-American at the highest rate of unemployment and underemployment of any ethnic group in America, thereby, causing economic and emotional turmoil for most African-American families and communities.

The story of Africans and their descendants (African-Americans) in America is not the romantic immigrant story of people escaping to America from religious and political persecution. It is a story of a kidnapped people, being forced into an unpaid labor force and deliberately and systematically disconnected from their cultural roots. Because the story of the African-Americans is not an immigrant one, it should not be forgotten by Americans or African-Americans. Just like there are lingering effects of the Crusades on Christians and Muslims, the Holocaust on the Jewish community; there are lingering effects of American slavery and its aftermath on the African-American family and community.

When we stop to examine the history of the African-American family, we will begin to uncover layers of untold truths. The African contribution to mankind has been so distorted by American and European *scholars* that even Egypt is no longer a country in Africa, but is considered to be a part of the Middle

East. We as African-Americans have accepted this view of Africa and Africans and our disconnect is complete. However, if we can embrace our total African-American family history, we can reconnect to our African culture and begin to repair the psychological and social damage of American slavery on African-American intimate relationships.

Chapter 2

Prelude to the Mating Game

According to the following statistics, the African-American family is as bad off today as it has ever been. In America, the comparative divorce rates are 32% for African-Americans, 22% for Hispanics and 21% for whites. According to research regarding first marriages, 70% of African-American first marriages will end in divorce while 47% of white first marriages will end in divorce. And with 1/3 of divorced African-Americans remarrying, these rates help contribute to the 72% of African-American children being raised by single African-American women. It is my contention that the real story behind the above statistics, is the continuous impact of American slavery and its aftermath on the psyche of African-Americans and their intimate relationships.

Marriage Training

It seems to me that the best way to approach the improvement of African-American intimate relationships is to start at the beginning. It has been my observation, that most African-Americans are not socially or psychological prepared for married life. This seems to be the result of a lack of marital training which is contrary to the way that our ancestors approached the issue of marriage. To change this behavior, it will take a commitment on the part of present day African-Americans to embrace the African view of the family and to impart the reality of married life to their offspring. This would include instructions for both genders on the division of labor, finances and sexual matters. This would not have any immediate effect on the stability of the African-American family because it will take twenty to thirty years for their offspring to be in a position to put their training into effect and to pass it onto their offspring, however, as long as both African-American parents are on the same page with this, this would be a great step in the right direction in an effort to have an impact on the above statistics.

Today, the responsibility of the African-American parent(s) as the marriage trainer, especially in the area of sexual matters seems to be given only *lip service*. See the top 10 responses to the question of sexual information sources in Table 2-1. As with all Tables and Comments presented in this book, responses are among those taken from a sample group that participated in the administration of the Adamore's Relationship Questionnaire (ARQ).

TABLE 2-1

What are the sources of your information concerning sexual matters?

Single African-American Women

Ages 22-28	Ages 29-36	Ages 37-43
1) Friends	1) Experience	1) Experience
2) Experience	2) Friends	2) Friends
3) Parent(s)	3) Doctor	3) Magazines/Books
4) Magazines/Books	4) Magazines/Books	4) Doctor
5) School	5) Parent(s)	5) Relatives
6) Doctor	6) Relatives	6) Parent(s)
7) Relatives	7) School	7) School
8) Television	8) Television	8) Television
9) Movies	9) Movies	9) Church
10) Church	10) Church	10) Movies

Single African-American Men

Ages 22-28	Ages 29-36	Ages 37-43
1) Experience	1) Experience	1) Experience
2) Friends	2) Magazines/Books	2) Magazines/Books
3) Magazines/Books	3) Friends	3) Friends
4) Parent(s)	4) School	4) Doctor
5) Television	5) Television	5) Relatives
6) Movies	6) Doctor	6) Parent(s)
7) School	7) Parent(s)	7) Television
8) Relatives	8) Movies	8) School
9) Church	9) Relatives	9) Movies
10) Doctor	10) Church	10) Church

From Table 2-1, it seems that personal experience and friends are the most important sources of information on sexual matters for African-American men and women. It seems to me that this is where the American educational system, monitored by organized religious doctrine, plays its part in the children's experimentation with sexual behavior. With the age of puberty getting lower in America and peer pressure, the experimentation with sexual behavior is beginning to take place at the elementary school level and is carried on throughout their high school and college years. The lessons learned during this experimentation, both positive and/or negative, are carried by them into their adult intimate relationship(s).

Table 2-1, verifies that the African-American parent(s) are not the primary source of information on sexual matters and their influence seems to wane as the respondents get older. I believe that this is caused by the parent(s) not giving much usable information because of their fear of being seen as a hypocrite for telling their child/children not to do the same things that they did when they were their age. This adds to their offspring's lack of preparation for involvement in intimate relationship(s). There will be more about the parenting responsibilities of African Americans in Chapter 6.

11

An additional observation from Table 2-1 is the importance of magazines/books for both genders, however, I think that a gender distinction has to be made. With regards to African-American women, I think that they are into both magazines (Essence, Ebony, Seventeen) and books (romance novels) while African American men are only into magazines (Playboy, GQ, Penthouse). This may be reflective of the developmental differences between men and women, where the woman is into the emotional aspects of an intimate relationship and the man is into the sexual aspects of an intimate relationship.

The Search

The search for a mate can take place anytime during a person's adult lifetime because of singleness, breakups, divorce or death of a spouse, therefore, finding themselves alone, the search for a mate begins. The question then arises as to where do you go to meet someone of the opposite sex for entertainment, fun and companionship? The general consensus is to go to a place where there are a lot of people (men/women), music, dancing and drinking (lounge, bar, club). However, In *What Brothers Think, What Sistahs Know: The Real Deal on Love and Relationships,* coauthors Denene Miller and Nick Chiles (husband and wife), tells how based on their insecurities with each other, African-Americans will bad-mouth each other in these social settings. When this question was asked of our sample group, their 10 top responses are in Table 2-2.

TABLE 2-2

Where would you go to meet someone of the opposite sex?

Single African-American Women

Ages 22-28	Ages 29-36	Ages 37-43
1) School	1) Church	1) A Friend
2) A Friend	2) A Friend	2) Cultural Event
3) Church	3) School	3) Church
4) Recreational Event	4) Cultural Event	4) - Recreational Event - School
5) - Cultural Event - Party	5) Work	5) Work
6) Work	6) Recreational Event	6) Party
7) Mall	7) Party	7) Lounge
8) Supermarket	8) Mall	8) Supermarket
9) Lounge	9) Supermarket	9) Mall
10) ————	10) Lounge	10) ————

Single African-American Men

Ages 22-28	Ages 29-36	Ages 37-43
1) School	1) Cultural Event	1) A Friend
2) A Friend	2) School	2) Cultural Event
3) Recreational Event	3) Church	3) Party
4) Church	4) A Friend	4) Church
5) Cultural Event	5) Recreational Event	5) Recreational Event
6) Party	6) Party	6) Work
7) Work	7) Work	7) School
8) Mall	8) Mall	8) Supermarket
9) Supermarket	9) Supermarket	9) Lounge
10) Lounge	10) Lounge	10) Mall

13

In Table 2-2, seeking out your friend(s) to help you find someone of the opposite sex seems to take the highest priority among the listed alternatives. In *Marriage Problems in Africa*, author Dike Egwuonwu stated that if an African man was having problems finding a mate, he would seek the help of his parents, relatives or friends.

In *The Sistahs' Rules: Secrets for Meeting, Getting, and Keeping a Good Black Man*, author Denene Millner, felt that the workplace was a good place to meet Mr. Right, however, I do not think that African-American men think that this is a good idea because of the Sexual Harassment laws that apply to the workplace.

It seems that trying to meet someone of the opposite sex for entertainment, fun and companionship is a hit or miss proposition, with no guarantees. I feel that if a person just does the things that they like to do, instead of running from place to place trying to meet someone, then they might meet someone who might become a friend or Mr./Ms. Right.

When African-American men and women are seeking to meet someone of the opposite sex, if they see someone that interest them, what is it about the physical appearance of that someone, that gets their attention? The sample group's 10 top responses can be seen in Table 2-3.

TABLE 2-3

What is it about the physical appearance of someone of the opposite sex that gets your attention?

Single African-American Women

Ages 22-28	Ages 29-36	Ages 37-43
1) Smile	1) Smile	1) Smile
2) Eyes	2) Eyes	2) Eyes
3) Skin Color	3) Skin Color	3) Hands
4) Hair	4) Chest	4) Hair
5) Legs	5) Hair	5) Skin Color
6) Chest	6) Buttock	6) Buttock
7) Buttock	7) Hands	7) Legs
8) Hands	8 Legs	8) Chest
9) Groin Area	9) Groin Area	9) Feet
10) Feet	10) Feet	10) Groin Area

Single African-American Men

Ages 22-28	Ages 29-36	Ages 37-43
1) Eyes	1) Legs	1) Smile
2) Smile	2) Buttock	2) Buttock
3) Breast	3) Eyes	3) Eyes
4) Buttock	4) Smile	4) Legs
5) Legs	5) Breast	5) Breast
6) Skin Color	6) Skin Color	6) Hair
7) Hair	7) Hair	7) Skin Color
8) Hands	8) Hands	8) Hands
9) Feet	9) Feet	9) Groin Area
10) Groin Area	10) Groin Area	10) Feet

15

Drama and the Search for Mr./Mrs. Right:
Understanding the Cycle of Mistreatment

According to Table 2-3, an African-American man can get an African-American women's attention, regardless of her age, with a smile and eye contact. For an African-American woman, she can get the attention of an African-American man with a smile and her physical attributes. The Table also explains why, an African-American man will look behind, when he is walking.

Also in Table 2-3, it seems that *skin color* still plays a part in the decision making of African-Americans in the mating game. The issue of skin color among African-Americans dates back to American slavery, where as a result of the rape of African women, the lighter-skinned offspring were treated better than the darker-skinned offspring. The lighter-skinned African offspring became the "house niggers" and the darker-skinned African offspring became the "field niggers." If there was some transaction that had to take place between the slave owner and the Africans, the lighter-skinned African offspring would be used as a "go between." Soon, based on skin color, there was a social distinction made in the African community; the lighter the skin color, the higher the social status. In *The Color Complex: The Politics of Skin Color Among African Americans,* authors Kathy Russell, Midge Wilson and Ronald Hall, called the attitudes of African-Americans about skin color and features, which includes hair texture, nose shape and eye color, as a psychological fixation that led them to discriminate against each other.

This reality of skin color has caused African-American women to spend a vast amount of their collective income on hair straighteners and skin lightening creams in an effort to be acceptable in American culture. This fixation on skin color is imbedded in the American and European propaganda concerning the standard of female beauty. The standard of female beauty as light-skinned, long straight blond hair and blue eyes has been ingrained in the people where American and European influence has penetrated their cultures. This can be seen in the number of highly paid and well-educated Africans and African-American men, who have married light-skinned American, European and African-American women instead of the dark-skinned women of African ancestry.

Also, in *The Color Complex,* authors Kathy Russell, Midge Wilson and Ronald Hall, indicated that African-American women were interested in skin color because (1) they found it attractive, (2) of her imagination regarding the skin color of the child/children that they would produce and (3) her concern about what type of competition she might encounter in trying to "catch" this man.

As regards the issue of skin color for African-American men, they will tell you that they do not have an issue with it, however, I believe that African-American men have consciously or unconsciously interchanged the American standard of beauty with an African-American standard of beauty which includes light-skinned and long-haired African-American women.

Once an African-American man or woman has seen someone of the opposite sex that strikes their fancy, the question is, who will make an attempt to create a chance encounter? There seems to be an agreed *general consensus* that the man should make the first move and the woman should then respond. This was verified when the sample group was asked who made the first move to create a chance encounter and 73% of single African-American men stated that they made the first move while 77% of single African-American women stated that they did *not* make the first move. From the following comments of the sample group, we might be able to get some insight as to the rationale behind this behavior?

Comments - Making the first move to create a chance encounter

Single African-American Men (Ages 22-28)

Yes   -I would introduce myself and try to find out what we have in common.

-If I see someone I think could be special, I do not want to let her slip away.

-I make the first (move) because I am a male. The society we live in, has a set of unwritten rules. One of the unwritten rules is the man should make the first move. Furthermore, most females expect the male to make the first move.

-Because someone else might come along and take them away or that person might (be) interested in you and might be afraid to approach you.

Single African-American Women (Ages 22-28)

No   -Because I'm very shy and I believe that if I make the first move, the other individual will consider me to be easy.

-No, because I am not a very assertive person in that area.

-Because I think I should be approached first, it is only lady like.

-I've often felt that men are intimidated by aggressive women. Also, I would consider myself as "old-fashion" in a sense.

-I have always been a very shy person, so I'll basically want to be approached. Also, because of my fear of rejection.

Single African-American Men (Ages 29-36)

Yes   -I would like to think that I do indeed make the first move, but the response depends entirely on the first impression I get from the individual (like a smile).

-If I see someone I like and think they're interested in me, I'll try (to) start a conversation.

-I let the female know I'm serious. I'm looking for some kind of commitment.

18

Comments - Making the first move to create a chance encounter

Single African-American Women (Ages 29-36)

No -I don't feel comfortable with confronting males or making passes. However, I will make the first move in starting a conversation.

-Don't want to give the wrong impression, such as I'm desperate for a man.

-Cannot take rejection.

-I do not want to feel that I am being pushy. But I do build a friendship first.

-If a woman is too forward, she can be taken for granted. Also, making the first move can lead men to believe she would do anything he wants her to do.

Single African-American Men (Ages 37-43)

Yes -Yes, that way I can choose the time and place.

-If she is attractive - it is best to seize the moment.

-I let a lady know if she looks like what I like.

-I like being the aggressor.

Single African-American Women (Ages 37-43)

No -Too nervous - self-conscious.

-I'm not an aggressive person. If a man does not approach me, I'll never get to know him.

-I usually wait awhile before starting (a) relationship, due to the fact I (am) very shy around new people and (it) takes time for me to relax enough.

-I don't think it's a woman's place.

-I leave this decision to the opposite sex, if there is an attraction.

Drama and the Search for Mr./Mrs. Right:
Understanding the Cycle of Mistreatment

From the above comments, it seems that African-American women are reluctant to make the first move because of (1) a *fear of rejection*, (2) being seen as too aggressive/easy and (3) social norms. Although the African-American man is making the first move, he too is subject to the fear of rejection because it is the African-American woman who makes the decision as to whether to continue or discontinue (reject) the encounter. Therefore, the woman controls the situation and limits her exposure to rejection. Fear of rejection is one of the main negative outcomes of teenage dating.

The fear of rejection is tied to one's self-esteem, it is a feeling of not being accepted, cared for or loved. We must understand that nobody really gets over being rejected. However, your worth as a person is not based on anyone's approval or rejection but based on the fact that you are worthy because of your existence as a human being. In order to deal with the fear of rejection, (1) we have to accept the fact that rejection is real and (2) that we reject as well as we are rejected.

The American society appears to be interested on everyone getting an education, however, it seems that when it comes to the two greatest events in a human's life, marriage and child rearing, there is no educational preparation for the individuals that find themselves about to embark on these events. It seems that the individuals are left with an on-the-job training approach to success or failure in these endeavors. By following this method, it seems to me that African-Americans have *thrown the baby out with the bath water.* Without retaining the practice of marriage training, we have assisted in our own downfall.

Chapter 3

The Mating Game

Protocols of the Mating Game

The *mating game* is the process by which men and women engage in social activities (*dating*) to determine if they are suitable for a long-term intimate relationship. Dating takes place when the African-American woman consents to being entertained (wine and dine) by the African-American man. As stated by Ms. Brenda Pogue, owner of Mingles, Inc., an African-American dating service in Chicago, "the man will spend a minimum of $2,000.00 and up, in a year's time, in an effort to get to know a woman." In *The Sistahs' Rules: Secrets for Meeting, Getting, and Keeping a Good Black Man*, author Denene Millner, acknowledges the concerns that African-American women have about the financial abilities of African-American men.

There are two major factors underpinning dating in America (1) *sexuality* and (2) *materialism*. These factors seem to have entered the African-American mating game and are acted out in the gender-based concepts I call, *objective* and *agenda*. African-American men have an *objective* and African-American women have an *agenda*. These concepts are continuously being acted out by African-American men and women throughout the mating game and marriage.

What is meant by the concept that African-American women have an *agenda* is that when the African-American woman starts dating, her immediate goal (wants/needs) is to be entertained, while she tries to determine if the African-American man is a good candidate for a long-term intimate relationship, which will lead to marriage, children and beyond.

While what is meant by the concept that African-American men have an *objective* is that when the African-American man starts dating, his immediate goal (wants/needs) is to obtain sexual gratification.

Once dating starts, a third factor underpinning dating is played out, the *unspoken expectation*. The unspoken expectation is the anticipation that the man will use his money for entertainment and gifts (the agenda) and that the woman will be forthcoming with sexual activity (the objective).

Mating Game - Phase I

Once the African-American woman has agreed to some social activity (date), the mating process begins. Although when we are talking about dating we are usually talking about single individuals, however, some attention should also be given to dating that involves single parents. Of the sample group, 37% of the single African-American women and 32% of the single African-American men stated that *they had a child or children from a previous relationship or marriage*. This would seem to complicate the dating situation because of the need for child/children care while dating is taking place. The main issue seems to be who would pay for the child/children care? I would think that the cost of the child/children care should be on the person who has custody of the child/children. This cost should not just be put on the man unless he is the custodial parent.

Also the custodial parent should let the admirer know as soon as possible that they have a child/children and the situation with the birth mother or father. This will allow the admirer to make an informed decision as to whether she or he wants to continue the relationship.

After the first date, what is it about your *date*, that you would take into consideration for continuing the dating relationship? The top 7 responses of the sample group are in Table 3-1.

TABLE 3-1

After the first date, what is it about a member of the opposite sex, that you will take into consideration for continuing the relationship?

Single African-American Women

Ages 22-28	Ages 29-36	Ages 37-43
1) Physical Appearance	1) Physical Appearance	1) Physical Appearance
2) Education	2) Education	2) Vibes
3) -Job	3) Vibes	3) Education
-Vibes		
4) Sexual Attraction	4) Job	4) Job
5) Religion	5) Religion	5) Sexual Attraction
6) Car	6) Sexual Attraction	6) Religion
7) —————	7) Car	7) Car

Single African-American Men

Ages 22-28	Ages 29-36	Ages 37-43
1) Physical Appearance	1) Physical Appearance	1) Physical Appearance
2) Sexual Attraction	2) Sexual Attraction	2) Sexual Attraction
3) Education	3) Vibes	3) Vibes
4) Vibes	4) Education	4) Job
5) Job	5) Job	5) Education
6) Religion	6) Religion	6) Car
7) Car	7) Car	7) Religion

Table 3-1 shows that African-American men and women will use personal attributes that can be observed or that can be easily determined, in making a decision to continue a dating relationship.

When dating is continued, the issue of sexual activity arises. Sex in the dating relationship can be either pleasurable or problematic.

When the sample group was asked about their sexual activity, 71% of single African-American men stated that they initiated the first sexual activity while 88% of single African-American women stated that they did *not* initiate the first sexual activity. Maybe the following comments from the sample group, could shed some light on this behavior.

Comments - The initiation of first sexual activity
Single African-American Men (Ages 22-28)

Yes   -When there is (an) urge and I'm comfortable with the person, I will initiate the sexual contact.

-Most females seem to feel uncomfortable initiating first sexual contact for fear of the impression it may give.

No   -Fear of rejection.

-When someone is ready to become sexually involved, they usually make it known.

-I'll wait until she's ready, then let her make the first move.

-She might feel that I am only after her body and she might feel offended.

Single African-American Women (Ages 22-28)

No   -Because of the ways of the world (aids-casual sex-vices-etc.). I carefully evaluate my partner and limit sexual contact until I am very sure of my partner's ethics, morals, habits, etc.

-I'm not aggressive. I feel it's the man's place to be the first to make sexual passes.

-It makes women seem loose.

-Some men might feel that if you're too quick to initiate sexual contact, you are therefore

Comments - The initiation of first sexual activity

Single African-American Women (Ages 22-28) (Contd.)

No   trying to give it away and therefore, there must be something wrong with it.

-I just don't think its lady like. I guess it has a lot to do with the way I was brought up.

-I generally prefer the male to initiate, which in turn gives me the opportunity to accept or (deny).

Single African-American Men (Ages 29-36)

Yes   -I like to play it by ear but usually I start it.

-I let the woman guide me to what she wants and how fast it should occur.

-Once she begins to feel comfortable with me, she will let me know and we go for it.

No   -Sexual contact has receded on my list of priorities.

-I am a person who is patient and believes that woman (is) also wanting the sexual relation to start.

Single African-American Women (Ages 29-36)

No   -I do not want to appear as being forward or give the impression that sex is all I am interested in.

-Because of my religious background, I try to avoid fornication as much as possible.

-I feel that your partner should. I kind of have old fashion values.

-I am a very cautious person. I find out what he is about, where his values lie. I investigate a man first.

-I feel that when sexual contact is initiated before disclosing, sharing and expression of trust must occur or the priorities will be confused by both parties.

<u>Comments - The initiation of first sexual activity</u>

Single African American Men (Ages 37-43)

Yes   -But only if I feel that the time is right. Usually I can tell by the women's hints, suggestions and body language. It is all in the timing.

           -I guess its just being a male - and it's expected.

           -Because I like the feeling of conquest.

No   -If she wants me, she (will) normally let me know.

           -I wouldn't want the feeling of rejection.

Single African American Women (Ages 37-43)

No   -Not anymore, since there's AIDS floating around.

           -Males initiate the first sexual contact.

           -I would not want the other person to think I am a free agent.

Here again, there is a general consensus that the man should make the first move and then the woman should respond. For African-American men, this again brings the fear of rejection into play and for African-American women, this brings into play (1) the fear of STD's, (2) fear of their reputation being smeared and/ or (3) violation of religious or family teachings. Yet, sexual activity goes on.

After the question on the initiation of sexual activity was asked, a follow-up question was asked as to how much time should pass in the dating relationship before they become sexually active? From the responses, 82% of African-American men were sexually active *within four months* of the start of a dating relationship while 71% of the African-American women were sexually active *within six months* of the start of a dating relationship.

The above discrepancy in reporting the beginning of sexual activity in the dating relationship, is in my opinion, an attempt on the part of African-American women to downplay their sexual proclivities.

When the sample group was asked about their use of birth control methods or devices, 58% of single African-American men and 48% of single African-American women said they did *not* use any birth control methods or devices. Their top 3 reasons for not using any birth control methods or devices can be found in Table 3-2.

TABLE 3-2

What are your reasons for not using any birth control methods or devices?

Single African-American Women

Ages 22-28	Ages 29-36	Ages 37-43
1) Not sexually active	1) Not sexually active	1) Medical Reasons
2) Sexual partner uses a birth control method or devices	2) Medical Reasons	2) Not sexually active
3) Medical Reasons	3) To have children	3) Sexual partner uses a birth control method or device

Single African-American Men

Ages 22-28	Ages 29-36	Ages 37-43
1) Limits sexual freedom	1) Sexual partner uses a birth control method or device	1) Limits sexual freedom
2) -Not satisfied with choices of methods or devices -Sexual partner uses a birth control method or device	2) Limits sexual freedom	2) Sexual partner uses a birth control method or device
3) ————————	3) Emotional feelings for sexual partner	3) Not satisfied with choices of methods or devices

27

As gleaned from Table 3-2, it seems that when African-American women are sexually active, their main reasons for *not* using any birth control methods or devices are: (1) their sexual partner uses a birth control method or device or (2) because of medical reasons; whereas when African-American men are sexually active, they are *not* using any birth control methods or devices (i.e., condoms - 90% effective against pregnancy and/or STD's) because (1) it limits their sexual freedom or (2) their sexual partner uses a birth control method or device.

In the above scenario, it seems that both African-American men and women are taking risks with pregnancy and/or STD's by leaving the responsible for the use of birth control methods or devices in the hands of their partners. This is putting both of their futures at risk. What seems to be the biggest problem is that the African-American man does not want to use any birth control method or device during sexual activity and their sexual partners are allowing them to do it. This type of behavior leads to pregnancy and the spread of STD's. African-American men and women *must* remember that the use of condoms keeps them in control of their future (the timing of their passage into parenthood) and minimizes the spread of STD's.

The failure to use any birth control method or device could result in pregnancy within the dating relationship. When that happens and the pregnancy is *known* to both partners, expectations arise which may or may not be realized. The top 3 reactions of both genders to the pregnancy of the African-American woman within the dating relationship are presented in Table 3-3.

28

TABLE 3-3

What should a female *Special Friend* do when she becomes pregnant?

Single African-American Women

Ages 22-28	Ages 29-36	Ages 37-43
1) Do not marry, but raise the child with input from both parents	1) Have the child and raise it by herself	1) Have the child and raise it by herself
2) Get married, depending on special friend	2) Get married, depending on special friend	2) Get married, depending on special friend
3) Have the child and raise it by herself	3) Do not marry, but raise the child with input from both parents	3) Do not marry, but raise the child with input from both parents

Single African-American Men

Ages 22-28	Ages 29-36	Ages 37-43
1) Do not marry, but raise the child with input from both parents	1) Do not marry, but raise the child with input from both parents	1) Get married, depending on special friend
2) Get married, depending on special friend	2) Get married, depending on special friend	2) Have the child and raise it by herself
3) Have the child and raise it by herself	3) Have an abortion	3) Do not marry, but raise the child with input from both parents

29

Table 3-3 points out some realities that have a major impact on the African-American community and are being played out in African-American dating relationships. It seems that (1) pregnancy is no longer an immediate consideration for African-American marriages and (2) that abortion is not a consideration for African-Americans women. These realities along with teenage pregnancies are the major reasons for the majority of African-American children being parented by single African-American women. This is seen as a direct result of the disconnect from African values concerning marriage and childbirth and leads to the possible conflict among African-American men and women.

When there is a pregnancy within the dating relationship, how should the man deal with the pregnancy? The top 3 reactions of both genders as to how the African-American man should deal with the pregnancy are presented in Table 3-4.

TABLE 3-4

What should a male *Special Friend* do when his female *Special Friend* becomes pregnant?

Single African-American Women

Ages 22-28	Ages 29-36	Ages 37-43
1) Do not marry, but provide financial support for the child	1) Get married, depending on special friend	1) Get married, depending on special friend
2) Do not marry, but share in the raising of the child	2) Do not marry, but share in the raising of the child	2) Do not marry, but share in the raising of the child
3) Get married, depending on special friend	3) Do not marry, but provide financial support for the child	3) Do not marry, but provide financial support for the child

TABLE 3-4 (Contd.)

What should a male *Special Friend* do when his female *Special Friend* becomes pregnant?

Single African-American Men

Ages 22-28	Ages 29-36	Ages 37-43
1) Do not marry, but provide financial support for the child	1) - Do not marry, but provide financial support for the child - Do not marry, but share in the raising of the child	1) Do not marry, but share in the raising of the child
2) Do not marry, but share in the raising of the child	2) Get married, depending on special friend	2) Do not marry, but provide financial support for the child
3) Get married, depending on special friend	3) ———————	3) Get married, depending on special friend

Table 3-4 points out that in the case of pregnancy within the dating relationship, the African-American man is expected to (1) provide financial support, (2) participate in the raising of the child and/or (3) get married. Evidence has shown that most

African-American men are not taking on their rightful parenting and financial responsibilities. As regards providing child support, African-American men tend to think that (1) the child is not theirs, (2) if they are not getting anything (sex), they are not giving anything (money) and/or (3) the money that is given to the birth mother, will not be spent on the child or children. This intensifies the problems concerning child rearing in the African-American community.

It seems that here again, is an area of conflict between African-American men and women because African-Americans do not seem to see childbirth as a continuation of the family and only gives "lip service" to the idea that they are our representation into the future.

As the dating relationship begins to develop, changes start to take place. It would be interesting to know who attempts to include trust and a sharing of feelings into the dating relationship? When this question was asked of the sample group, 68% of single African-American men stated that they *did* make the first attempt to include trust and a sharing of feelings into the relationship while 64% of single African-American women stated that they *did not* make the first attempt to include trust and a sharing of feelings into the relationship. The rationale for their behavior can be found in the following comments.

Comments - Attempt to include trust and a sharing of feelings into the relationship

Single African-American Men (Ages 22-28)

Yes   -I am usually the one that shows my compassion first.
-Because I express trust and honesty and require it in a relationship.
-If I show that I can be open with her, then she can be open with me.

Comments - Attempt to include trust and a sharing of feelings into the relationship

Single African-American Women (Ages 22-28)

No   -Because I don't like getting my feelings hurt.

-I don't want to express my feelings until I know he has (shown) some kind of sign of   personal feelings.

-I sometimes have a hard time expressing my feelings although I do give trust.

-I usually hold back my feelings since I do not want to take the chance of getting hurt, but once I feel comfortable, I begin to open up.

-Most men do not open up to any woman unless they trust you and that takes a long time, so I leave that up to whoever the person is.

Single African-American Men (Ages 29-36)

Yes   -That way I will know how interested they are in me.

-I like control.

-Once I have liked everything about the lady, I would want to let her know so that she can help me in some emotional things.

Single African-American Women (Ages 29-36)

No   -I am very untrusting.

-I like to feel men out before I commit any time or feeling(s). Also, I want to know up front if he is interested in me.

-I got my feelings hurt and will never do it again.

Single African-American Men (Ages 37-43)

Yes   -I am an extremely soft spoken and honest man. I don't like games, so I try to let this be known from the beginning but trust is earned and a number of women don't trust men much (with good reason, I might add) so it's a difficult task.

Single African-American Women (Ages 37-43)

No   -No comment.

33

Based on the comments from the sample group, *trust* seems to be the major issue in the dating relationship. Trust is having *faith* that another person will not cause you harm. It seems that both African-American men and women are not trusting of each other. This mistrust is felt to be the result of (1) learning and/or (2) the interactions experienced during teenage dating. In most dating relationships, trust that is initially given based on *faith*, is usually trampled on or destroyed by either partner. It seems that when a person is found not to be trustworthy in a particular situation, it is assumed that they are not trustworthy in any situation. This may not always be true. Sometimes, when a breach of trust is recognized, the person can be remorseful. When this happens, there is another type of trust that comes into play, a type of trust that is *earned* based on a time period of positive interactions with that person. Also, the person who feels betrayed, has to be able to forgive the other person, not for that person's sake but for their own well-being.

After the question of attempting to include trust and a sharing of feelings into the dating relationship, a follow-up question was asked as to how much time should pass in the dating relationship before attempting to include trust and a sharing of feelings? From the responses, 78% of the single African-American men thought that *within four months* of the start of a dating relationship, there should be trust and a sharing of feelings while 77% of single African-American women thought that *within six months* of the start of a dating relationship, there should be trust and a sharing of feelings.

The top 7 ways to show your partner that you care can be seen in Table 3-5.

TABLE 3-5

In what ways do you let your *Special Friend* know that you care?

Single African-American Women

Ages 22-28	Ages 29-36	Ages 37-43
1) Tell him	1) Tell him	1) Tell him
2) Be affectionate, without sex	2) Be affectionate, without sex	2) Be affectionate, without sex
3) Send card	3) Send card	3) Dinner (In/Out)
4) Dinner (In/Out)	4) Dinner (In/Out)	4) Send card
5) Buy a gift	5) Buy a gift	5) Have sex
6) Send flowers	6) Have sex	6) Buy a gift
7) Have sex	7) Send flowers	7) Send flowers

Single African-American Men

Ages 22-28	Ages 29-36	Ages 37-43
1) Tell her	1) Tell her	1) Tell her
2) Be affectionate, without sex	2) Be affectionate, without sex	2) Dinner (In/Out)
3) Send card	3) Dinner (In/Out)	3) Be affectionate, without sex
4) Send flowers	4) Send card	4) Send flowers
5) Dinner (In/Out)	5) Buy a gift	5) Have sex
6) Buy a gift	6) Have sex	6) Send card
7) Have sex	7) Send flowers	7) Buy a gift

For those who would need some additional help with Table 3-5, here are some tips: (1) *always thank* him or her for whatever they do for you because they do not have to do it, (2) leave the card (for the men-always read and understand what the card is saying) in his or her briefcase, send it to his or her office, leave it on his or her car seat, under his or her pillow, etc. (3) in *The Sistah's Rules: Secrets for Meeting, Getting, and Keeping a Good Black Man,* author Denene Millner, suggests that African-American women should cook for African-American men (The Way to a Man's Heart Is Through a Great Plate of Greens), (4) buy a gift in his or her favorite color, and (5) be affectionate without sex by kissing and hugging, cuddling in bed or on the sofa, casual touching and holding hands.

Mating Game - Phase II

If the dating relationship has gone on for a while, the next step in the mating game is the intimate relationship. However, the beginning of the intimate relationship seems to be a nebulous event, because all of the outward behavioral signs of its existence are similar to dating behavior. Therefore, we have to assume that a couple is in an intimate relationship when they tell you that they are (1) "in a serious relationship," (2) "moving to the next level" and/or (3) "we're still together." Again this is nebulous. What I think is meant by these statements, is that a psychological shift has taken place within one or both partners and the intimate relationship has begun.

In general, when men and women meet, they enter into dating with their priorities placed on the sexual and material aspects of dating. This continues until a psychological shift takes place and then there is movement from the sexual and material aspects of dating, to either the (1) sexual/material and *emotional* aspects, (2) the sexual/material, emotional and *mental* aspects or (3) to the sexual/material, emotional, mental and *spiritual* aspects of an intimate relationship. Sometimes the psychological shift does not take place and the relationship is fixated in the sexual and material aspects of dating. However, when the psychological shift has been made, it is hoped that the emotional, mental or spiritual aspects of the relationship are brought into balance with or surpass the sexual and material aspects of the relationship.

As the intimate relationship begins to develop, there are possible challenges that the couple might face, which could put the mating process in jeopardy. These possible challenges come from within and/or outside of the relationship. The following is just a sample of the possible challenges that might occur.

Possibility #1-Parent(s) - The parent(s) is the person(s) who might have some positive/negative influence on the mating process. When the sample group was asked if their parent('s) opinion of their *Special Friend* had any effect on their relationship with their *Special Friend,* 67% of single African-American men and 63% of single African-American women stated that their parent('s) opinion had *no influence.*

This is contrary to African family values. In traditional African societies it is felt that since the parents are the ones that have raised and taught the child (male or female), they know the child better than he or she knows his or herself. Therefore, the parent's opinion concerning a mate is paramount and trusted.

Possibility #2-Friends - Friends are another group of people who might have some positive/negative influence on the mating process. As regards the opinion of their friends, 72% of single African-American men and 75% of single African-American women stated that their friend's opinion had *no influence.*

I find it difficult to believe the responses of African-American women to the above possibilities one and two because of the *sister's network.* The sister's network consists of the mother and girlfriends of single or married African-American women, who provides her with practical and emotional support: such as

37

babysitting, exchange of outfits, excuses, etc. Therefore, I find it hard to believe that African-American women do not accept the opinions of the members of their sister network.

Possibility #3-Disclosures - Sometime in the mating process there will be personal conversations where disclosures are made. It has been my experience that African-American men will disclose personal information earlier in the relationship than African-American women. This early and uneven rate of disclosure by African-American men puts them in a vulnerable position. It seems incumbent upon the African-American man to get as much personal information as he is giving out. Hopefully, this will minimize any surprise disclosures by African-American women because the question was never asked.

Possibility #4-Materialism - As the African-American man continues to receive sexual gratification, an issue that seems to present itself, is the requirement for the man to share or pay for the female's financial obligations. When the sample group was asked about this matter, 54% of single African-American men felt that the man *should not* share or pay for the female's financial obligations while 60% of single African-American women felt that the man *should* share or pay for the female's financial obligations. From the responses, it seems that both African-American men and women have concerns about this issue. From the following comments, maybe we can get some insight on the thought processes of both genders, concerning this issue.

Comments - Male sharing or paying for a female's personal expenses
       Single African-American Women (Ages 22-28)
Yes   -I don't think that he should support me now, but if I need help with something, I should be able to come to him and get it.
      -If he can't provide for her, he should not see her.

Comments - Male sharing or paying for a female's personal expenses

Single African-American Women (Ages 22-28)(Contd.)

Yes -That's part of what man is supposed to do.

-Because he has to win the female over.

-If a male friend offers to pay for certain financial obligations of his special friend, then that is between them. Otherwise, it shouldn't be something that is demanded or expected.

No -After marriage then that is the couple's job to work together.

-Unless you are getting married, then the guy should never pay the female's financial obligations, he can offer to help in times of crisis, but those offers should always be turned down.

-Female should be independent financially and otherwise. A female should not believe a male will take care of her just because he considers her to be "special."

-I feel that this special friend did not make the bills, so don't expect that he or she should share or pay. One should always try to be financially independent. What if the person starts paying then walks out?

Single African-American Men (Ages 22-28)

No -There shouldn't be financial obligations unless the couple are married or have a child.

-I feel that a person should not pay each other bills until marriage or until living together.

-She (has) to learn to make her own money.

-I have enough bills of my own.

Yes -Men will have to end up doing it anyway.

-Make sure that there is a strong commitment.

-I believe that (is) the man's job or role.

- I believe if you are going out together, the expenses can be shared, but financial obligations are separate until marriage or engagement. But if she needs help, she should let it be known and ask him with an offer to repay him even if he doesn't accept repayment the offer would be sufficient.

Comments - Male sharing or paying for a female's personal expenses

Single African-American Men (Ages 22-28) (Contd.)

Yes   -Only when there is a need and (the) special friend can't pay (their) financial obligations.

Single African-American Women (Ages 29-36)

Yes   -I feel that a man not living with his female, should help her out a "little."

-If you haven't decided to get married yet, then the male special friend helps voluntarily, not because it's expected.

-If the relationship was a financial one, then immediate but if the special friend cares about the female, then he'll do it without being asked.

-If it could be established early in the relationship, that an individual is not trying to be manipulative, financial assistance shouldn't present a problem.

-If he sees that his special friend is in a bind, he should help out.

No   -No one is obligated to pay for another's expenses unless it's something the person wants to do.

-You have to make sure that the person wants you and not your money. Money can't buy you love.

-Because I am very self-reliant and don't really depend on a man.

-I don't believe men should have to pay for bills I have created.

-Unless you are in an exclusive relationship, your financial obligations are your own.

Comments - Male sharing or paying for a female's personal expenses

Single African-American Men (Ages 29-36)

No   -There should be a full commitment between two people before financial obligations should be taken on.

-I will help only if I want to.

-Your special friend will probably be working and should take care of herself.

-I absolutely refuse to subsidize the income of a woman I'm involved with. This has cost me several important relationships and many opportunities. I stand fast by the belief that the only way to know that the woman is interested in you and not the income subsidy, is not to provide an income subsidy.

Yes   -Her responsibilities are not yours, but if you would enjoy helping, that's fine.

-If it (is) necessary, this should be worked on in correspondence with your special friend. It should never become the basis of the relationship.

-If you have a relationship with a person and you visit or live there regularly, it's only reasonable to help pay some expenses.

-If the male can share her bed, why not the bills.

-If we are going to be together then that means emotionally, physically and financially.

Single African-American Women (Ages 37-43)

Yes   -Depends on what obligations he wants from the female.

-If you and your friend are spending time together, almost like a marriage, yes he should help financially.

-I feel if he sees I am trying to make it on my own, Help Please.

-Only when the friend has financial problems.

41

Comments - Male sharing or paying for a female's personal expenses

Single African-American Women (Ages 37-43) (Contd.)

-To show good faith and respect for the person.

Yes   -I'm too independent to have anyone pay for my financial obligations.

-There is no need to share or pay for my expenses unless we are married. I do not agree with living together.

-The female is totally responsible for her own financial obligations. In case of marriage, the relationship should be built on equity.

-I can financially take care of myself.

-I feel the friend should not be obligated to share or made to pay anything, unless he feels the need to or wants to.

Single African-American Men (Ages 37-43)

No   -I believe a couple should be married before sharing financial obligations.

-Until a live together or marriage commitment is made, everyone should take care of their own obligations.

-Her money problems are hers. I shouldn't have to pay for her mistakes.

-If there isn't a joint effort in creating this obligation, then why should this significant other take on this responsibility or obligation.

Yes   -If you care, you should show it.

-You must carefully assess the situation and make sure you're not getting used.

-If we're together, we should take care of each other.

-I believe in helping, but that should not be the primary thrust of a woman's attention.

The high percentage of single African-American men who believe that they should share or pay the financial obligations of single African-American women might be caused by so many African-American men being raised in a single female household and thereby experiencing the financial plight of their female parent. He may be willing to *help out* (e.g., emergency house/car repairs, babysitting fees, dry-cleaning bills, etc.), however, when his financial assistance calls for paying (1) credit card bills, (2) rent/house payments and/or (3) car payments; because he has his own set of financial obligations, he may be unable or unwilling to share or pay for her financial obligations and he is then held accountable by the African-American woman for his lack of financial assistance.

Possibility #5 - Nights Out - One situation that might cause problems within the intimate relationship is the partner's desire to have a night out with their friends. What is considered to be the problem, is the fear that each partner has of their partner's single friends. The African-American woman's fear is that her mate's single friends are (1) taking him to places that a committed man should not go, (2) are still trying to hook him up with other women and/or (3) telling him to stay single.

On the other hand, the African-American men fear that his mate's single friends are (1) dogging him because they do not have a boyfriend, (2) they do not what her to stop spending quality time with them and/or (3) that they will do or say something that will sabotage their relationship.

Possibility #6 -Close relationship with opposite sex - When a partner has a close relationship with someone of the opposite sex; this could lead to conflict within the intimate relationship. The volatility of this issue was seen when the sample group was asked this question and 62% of single African-American men and 52% of single African-American women *were opposed to it*. The ambivalence of both genders toward this issue, is presented in their following comments.

Comments - Close relationship with the opposite sex
Single African-American Women (Ages 22-28)

No -Most of the time, friends of the opposite sex usually cause problems in the relationship unless they are friends of both partners.

-There are too many diseases.

-I don't believe that a person who has formerly been involved intimately with the opposite sex can afterwards be their friend.

-I don't believe in sharing.

-I feel threatened by them because they knew him before I did and also they might try to test him to see just how serious he is about me.

Yes -A true friendship never ends but relationships sometimes do.

-Because you and that friend must have some kind of trust, and if both of you trust each other, then there is no need to have fear.

-If the individual proves himself to be trustworthy, he should continue his friendships with females (excluding physical intimate relationship). I'm not a jealous individual and I will continue to have close relationships with other males. Male and females can remain friends without creating more (in) the relationship.

-Up to and including sex, provided he does it safely. If it is a factor that has been thoroughly discussed and agreed upon, then it should be o.k.

-One person cannot be everything to the other. Relationships (non-sexual) with other parties can allow that person other opportunities for growth and make him more interesting.

Comments - Close relationship with the opposite sex
     Single African-American Men (Ages 22-28)
No   -Because I am a jealous person.

-I don't think so because I feel that most males would use the female friend as a sexual partner when she comes to him for advice because she and her boyfriend are not getting along.

-Closeness with the opposite sex creates conditions that are conducive to multiple sex partners.

-I will not trust her friends.

-If what we have is that special, why would either of us continue to do so?

Yes   -A friend is a friend.

-Because each individual has their own life to live.

-If she wants to have close relationships with other males, that is fine, as long as I receive the same space and respect.

-As long as we're not married, we have the freedom to see and do whatever we want.

-If she was close to someone before, then I shouldn't be the one to terminate that friendship.

     Single African-American Women (Ages 29-36)
No   -Because that would destroy our relationship in the long run, because the trust that we built would be destroyed.

-If we're together in commitment, I feel there's no need for a close relationship with another female other than me.

-Too risky and generally people don't exercise discipline of their sexual desire.

-I choose to engage in a monogamous relationship, which involves mutual trust and open communication between two mutually consenting individuals. If this, cannot be achieved, then there cannot be a relationship at all.

Comments - Close relationship with the opposite sex
Single African-American Women (Ages 29-36)(Contd.)

Yes   -If the relationships are platonic, I will say yes. I would not appreciate him continuing to have sex during the course of our relationship.

-Friends with the opposite gender is healthy and sometimes needed. I encourage it.

-If not sexual.

-If they are friends that have been introduced to me as a friend, not as ex-sexual partners, then the friendship should continue.

-If this is what he chooses. I would never give up my close male friends for the reason that I am involved with someone.

Single African-American Men (Ages 29-36)

No   -Might get too involved.

-Too many things that can cause conflict, such as emotions, STD's, etc.

-I think she should work on one relationship at a time.

-One partner per customer.

-A special friend is someone who should be your own special love mate not anyone else's.

Yes.   -I don't own her.

-I don't feel threatened by her having a relationship with other men.

-You learn from your friends not school, textbook or parents.

-People should be free to do whatever it is that they want to do and not feel restricted about it.

Single African-American Women (Ages 37-43)

No   -My special friend. I do not permit him to have opposite sex friends. I've had too many bad experiences where I let my friend associate with the opposite sex.

-Because I do not wish to get AIDS from this person or any other sexually transmitted diseases.

-Never trust the opposite sex with your special friend.

-I believe in monogamous relationships.

Comments - Close relationship with the opposite sex
Single African-American Women (Ages 37-43) (Contd.)

Yes   -I would question his personality if he had no other close relationship.

-If he has close friends of the opposite sex, he should not be forced to give them up because he is my special friend.

-The nature and intellectual way is for both partners to keep their friends and this keeps the relationship alive.

-Friends should always remain friends.

-One should always have friends of the opposite gender. It gives more balance to life.

Single African-American Men (Ages 37-43)

No   -Defeats the purpose of being a "special friend."

-Not if she's going to be with me.

-The word usage close relationship - means that it may develop into intimacy. Therefore, a certain respectful distance should be maintained.

-Because it may lead into another relationship with other persons.

-Too hazardous and it dilutes relationships.

-I should be enough for her.

Yes   -Yes I do because they are still a friend regardless of sex.

-Friends are friends - their sex makes (or at least to me) no difference. I'd be a fool to believe that I could meet all of her needs, so why should I get upset if she has male friends? That's unrealistic and grossly immature and unfair to both of us.

-Her life should expand not change abruptly because of a relationship. If there's no trust - you don't have anything.

Drama and the Search for Mr./Mrs. Right:
Understanding the Cycle of Mistreatment

From the comments of the sample group, the concern about a partner's close relationship with someone of the opposite sex, is about trust and the nature of the relationship between the opposite sex person and their partner? In *What Brothers Think, What Sistahs Know About Sex: The Real Deal on Passion, Loving and Intimacy,* co-authors Denene Millner and Nick Chiles, commented on the fear that each partner has about their partner's friendship with single members of the opposite sex. They state that this fear comes from the knowledge that each partner has of the sexual tendencies of their own gender. This adds to the fear that some of these opposite sex "friendships" are in reality "sexual attractions" that have not been consummated. Also, because some men and women have experienced "sexual attraction" friendships with the opposite sex, both genders have internal conflicts when they have to deal with a partner who has a close relationship with someone of the opposite sex.

Something that also has to be taken into consideration is the fact that most people have had a life prior to meeting their present mate and therefore may have friends from the opposite sex. If the opposite sex friend is introduced into the new relationship as a friend, then a friend should remain a friend until proven otherwise.

Possibility #7 - Child/Children from a previous relationship or marriage - What has been previously indicated about the sample group, is that 37% of the single African-American women and 32% of the single African-American men have a child or children from a previous relationship or marriage.

Within this group, 35% of the single African-American women and 59% of the single African-American men reported that the presence of a child or children from a previous relationship or marriage, *had an effect on their relationship with their Special Friend.*

48

Some of the issues that exist for either partner because of the presence of a child or children from a previous relationship or marriage are (1) the acceptance of the partner's child or children, by the other partner, (2) acceptance of the other partner by the child or children (3) the reaction of the birth mother or father, to the presence of another adult in their child or children's life, (4) differing parenting abilities and styles, (5) economic support for the child or children from a previous relationship or marriage and (6) the nature of the relationship between the birth parents. When there is a negative response to any of these issues, it could lead to conflict within the mating process.

Possibility #8 - Violence in the Mating Game - One of the least talked about subjects in the mating game is the violent/abusive behavior (i.e., biting, kicking, slapping, date rape, etc.) that takes place. I believe that the violent/abusive behavior is caused by the factors of (1) *the concept of objective,* (2) *the concept of agenda* and (3) *the unspoken expectation.* The *unspoken expectation* (concerns about sex and money) is the link between the concepts of *objective* (the man seeking sexual activity) and *agenda* (the woman seeking entertainment and gifts). As long as everyone is on the same page, everything is ok, however, if they are not on the same page, animosity and/or violent/abusive behavior might result. When a man has entertained and bought gifts for a woman and sexual activity is not forthcoming, according to the unspoken expectation, he feels justified in taking his sexual gratification by force. I believe that more attention should be given to these three factors and their impact on violence in the mating game. More information about violent/abusive behavior can be found in Chapter 5.

I know that some of you are thinking, what is happening to the romance? If there are any romantic feelings in the mating game, it does not seem to last long beyond the wedding ceremony. Maybe what is being perceived as romance is just a feeling of lust, the urge to satisfy one's sexual desire with a particular person. If the sexual encounter is pleasurable, it will invoke further encounters. These feelings of lust can be misinterpreted as love and this loving feeling is then used to move the relationship forward.

Chapter 4

The Decisions

As the intimate relationship continues and the partners begin to learn more about each other, the relationship begins to approach what seems to be two main decision making periods; (1) twelve months and (2) eighteen months (women) - two years or longer (men), where the issues of living together and/or marriage is raised and decided.

Living Together

It seems that once the twelve-month decision making period has been reached the question of possible living together arises. When the sample group was asked if they would consider a living together arrangement with their Special Friend, 54% of single African-American men stated that they *would* while 55% of single African-American women stated that they *would not* consider a living together arrangement. There seems to be a large number of African-American men and women who have some positive and/ or negative concerns about this issue. This is reflected in the following comments from the sample group.

Comments - Preference for living together

Single African-American Women (Ages 22-28)

No   -There is no commitment.

-Because living together is not advisable because of religious reasons.

-If you can have sex with me, you can marry me! Also, it would keep my mother from having a massive heart attack.

-At this point in my life, I am really too self oriented to live with someone that I'm sexually involved with.

Comments - Preference for living together
Single African-American Women (Ages 22-28) (Contd.)

No   -My grandmother said never live with a man-if you feel you can live together, you can be married.

Yes   -If we both have worked together to earn things and if it is in both of our names.

-Yes, only if the feelings were mutual and heading in a positive direction such as marriage.

-Just for financial reasons.

-I love him enough to share my life.

-If I believe the relationship is a close relationship and the relationship has very strong characteristics of being long-lasting.

-We're already discussed the possibility of marriage and it would be better to see how things may go beforehand.

Single African-American Men (Ages 22-28)

Yes   -Because if I love my special friend, I want to spend my time with her.

-I think it's a good way to become closer.

-The sexual experience will make the difference on whether or not you're ready to get married.

-If we continue to get closer over a period of time, that would be the natural next step.

No   -Not until marriage

-I'm too moody.

-Living together is nice temporarily but quickly turns into an invasion of privacy.

-I'd rather be alone and have my freedom.

-Because right now that would be like a marriage, because you would be expected to come straight home and be together. This is something I'm not ready for, not until I get married.

-I believe you should be married first or at least planning to be, because it can cause more harm than good in most cases.

Comments-Preference for living together

Single African-American Women (Ages 29-36)

No   -I came from a Christian background. My moral values would not allow it. I also like commitments. I do not believe in playing wife for free.

-I like living alone.

-I don't believe that living together is ok until after marriage or at least engagement.

-Well, I was raised that if you live together, you might as well get married. It's disrespectful to me.

-Marry me first.

Yes   -If two people truly care for each other, but certain problems prohibit them from getting married (finances or job security), then maybe living together is better.

-To check out their everyday pattern of daily living.

-After I am financially independent.

-It would allow us to spend more time together.

-If the commitment is there, the relationship can be permanent.

Single African-American Men (Ages 29-36)

Yes   -To see if you can get along before getting married.

-A prelude to marriage.

-We find it to be more economical.

-If we're compatible and we love each other, it would be the best thing to do.

-We would be able to see more of each other's habits and save money toward our future.

No   -(Neither) she nor myself are ready for this arrangement.

-Too much attachment, it's the same as marriage but without the contract.

-I like having space between myself and a special friend.

-I am totally against it because of my religious beliefs.

-I don't want to live with anyone that I'm not married to. You can visit for a while but some point in time, you have to go home.

Comments- Preference for living together

Single African-American Women (Ages 37-43)

No   -I couldn't tolerate that much closeness.

-I believe in separate but equal space and time away from each (other) unless married.

-I believe that a certain amount of respect will be lost.

-If two people care enough about themselves and their relationship and they want to live together - they should get married for the security of both parties.

-Never. From experience, the male wants the woman to act as a wife and he wants to act as though he is single.

-If you can live with them, you can get married.

Yes   -Live with him for a while to see if this is the relationship you really want and to find out what kind of man you might be marrying in the future.

-More accurate assessment of compatibility.

-Because I have strong feelings for him and want to be with him.

-I don't want to get married.

Single African-American Men (Ages 37-43)

Yes   -If I think we can live together, we should.

-To see how well we get along together.

-To live together, is to know more about her.

-It may be worth a try, the result of which could be very rewarding.

-I enjoy her company.

No   -I may as well get married.

-Everyone needs their own space. The Women's Movement has ruined the concept of home and family.

-I believe in marriage.

-I like my independence.

-All the advantages without the commitment. No Good.

The comments of the respondents who agree that a living together arrangement is a test before marriage, seems to echo the sentiments of co-authors Denene Millner and Nick Chiles, in *What Brothers Think, What Sistahs Know: The Real Deal on Love and Relationships*. In addition, I believe that the concepts of agenda and objective are still at play here. From the African-American woman's viewpoint, she will either enter a living together arrangement that she sees as a prelude to marriage or she will not enter into a living together arrangement until marriage. Either way is leading to a completion of the marriage item on her agenda.

As regards the African-American man, he sees a living together arrangement as a way to spend more time (sexual) with his partner or as a threat to his sexual freedom. Either way is leading to the continuation of his objective.

A living together arrangement is a risky business because both parties have something to lose in terms of time, emotions and finances. This is why, during this time, the real work of self-disclosure and compromise that is needed to provide a good foundation for the marital relationship, is not really done. The thought is either he or she will change or I will change him or her after we are married.

On the other hand, it seems that those who opt out of the living together arrangements, are not giving themselves, the best chance at having a good workable marriage. This is because all the reasons for not going through the living together arrangement is just delaying the experience of self-disclosure and compromise that will have to be done anyway after marriage, and then the cost of a breakup becomes higher in terms of time, emotions and finances. The breakup could lead to violent/abusive behavior.

In a follow-up question, would you consider a living together arrangement as an alternative to marriage, of the sample group, 40% of single African-American men and 27% of single African-American women stated that they *would consider a living together arrangement as an alternative to marriage.* These responses seem to indicate that there are a large percentage of African-American men and women who are willing to have a long-term committed relationship, without the marriage rituals.

The Marriage Decision

Whether the partners are in a living together arrangement or not, by the time that the relationship begins to approach the eighteen months (women) or the two years or longer (men) decision making period, the question of marriage is usually raised. In making the decision to marry, the general consensus that the man should make the first move and the woman should then respond is reversed, however, the concepts of agenda and objective remain the same. Also, hidden in this decision to marry is the *unspoken time frame* of the female partner, where the man *must* make a favorable response to the woman's marriage inquiry within the *unspoken time frame* or the relationship is ended. This presumes that both men and women are on the same page and in the same time zone, of course this is not always the case. Against this backdrop, the marriage decision is made.

In *The Sistahs' Rules: Secrets for Meeting, Getting, and Keeping a Good Black Man,* co-author Denene Millner, suggests how the African-American woman should approach the marriage issue. She suggests that after the couple has been in a committed relationship for about a year, then the African-American woman should approach the African-American man about his intentions for the future. If there is no positive response at the time, the African-American woman should give the African-American man at least two more years to make a decision. The African-American man has not been made aware that he has been placed on a time schedule.

If there is no commitment at the end of the African-American woman's time period, then she should give him an ultimatum with a choice: commit to marriage or we can continue to see each other and other people. Millner then states that because of the

African-American man's ego, he will not like to *share his woman* with another man and he will commit.

This approach to the marriage decision does not seem to be a reflection of any African values, religious or romantic ideology. With this approach, it seems like the concepts of objective and agenda are functioning at their best. It seems to verify my premise concerning human behavior: human beings create relationships when they try to get their *own* wants/needs met with or through another human being.

Whenever and however the issue of marriage is approached and dealt with, the question then arises as to what factors might lead the partners into making a decision to marry? See the top 8 responses of African-Americans to this question in Table 4-1.

TABLE 4-1
What factors would you take into consideration in making a decision to marry?

Single African-American Women

Ages 22-28	Ages 29-36	Ages 37-4
1) Love	1) Love	1) Love
2) Trust	2) Trust	2) Compatibility
3) Respect	3) Compatibility	3) Trust
4) Compatibility	4) Respect	4) Respect
5) Friendship	5) Friendship	5) Friendship
6) Financial Security	6) Financial Security	6) Personality
7) Personality	7) Sexual Attraction	7) Sexual Attraction
8) Education	8) Emotional Support	8) Financial Security

TABLE 4-1 (Contd.)
What factors would you take into consideration in making a decision to marry?

Single African-American Men

Ages 22-28	Ages 29-36	Ages 37-43
1) Love	1) Trust	1) Love
2) Trust	2) Love	2) Trust
3) Respect	3) Compatibility	3) Compatibility
4) -Friendship -Compatibility	4) -Respect -Friendship	4) Sexual Attraction
5) Personality	5) Sexual Attraction	5) Friendship
6) Financial Security	6) Personality	6) Respect
7) Sexual Attraction	7) Financial Security	7) Personality
8) ————	8) ————	8) Physical Appearance

In Table 4-1, it seems that *trust* is just as much of a primary consideration for marriage as is *love*. From my observation, as regards African-American women, the issues of trust and love seem to be centered around the man's sexual monogamy and for African-American men, the issues of trust and love seem to be centered around the fear that the woman will not be around if the man is not able to provide for her financially.

Nevertheless, when there is a marriage agreement (*engagement*), this signals the end of the search for Mr./Ms. Right and the beginning of the next step: marriage, the spiritual and legal extension of the mating process. All the attention is now focused on the wedding plans and the honeymoon. There is the romantic belief that all will be fine and life will be happy ever after.

Chapter 5

When Love Is Not Enough

With my years of studying conflict within mating/marital relationships and the counseling of men charged with domestic violence, I feel that there needs to be a better understanding of conflict other than the man as the perpetrator and the woman as the victim. I feel that an educational understanding of the *genesis of conflict* will reveal more about how to minimize the outbreak of violent/abusive behavior in mating/marital relationships than is presently understood.

In this chapter, I will explain the genesis of conflict as they apply to human beings in general, with some references that are exclusive to African-Americans. In Chapter 6, I will explain how to minimize conflict within intimate relationships.

Wants and Needs

Conflict *is a state of opposition*. Conflict exists in human interactions because of *unresolved wants/needs (mainly wants)*. A want is something that is *desired* and a need is something that is *required*. Even though a human infant (male or female) is born dependent on its parents or significant other(s) for its survival; the human infant is also born with capacities (brain, emotions and the five senses) and certain abilities that are geared toward its survival. An infant is also born with its own wants (to understand its environment) and needs (food, warmth, sleep) and not that of its parents or significant other(s).

As the infant grows to an adult and through his or her interaction with their environment, he or she learns to strive for more than just basic needs (food, clothing and shelter) but for

59

wants based on his or her gender as indicated by parents, the educational system, religion and the media. Also, the adult (male/female), learns that they need help from other human beings in order to obtain their wants/needs. This brings me to my premise concerning human behavior. I feel that the motivating force underpinning human behavior is wants/needs because (1) every human being has wants/needs, (2) every human being conducts their life in such a way as to get their own wants/needs met and (3) relationships are created because human beings are trying to get their *own* wants/needs met with or through another human being. These wants/needs are either conscious or unconscious to the human being. When human beings are not getting their wants/needs (*mainly wants*) met, there is conflict.

The Aftermath

It seems that as soon as the happy couple say "I Do, "something happens. It seems that the factors which lead African-American men and women to marry (see Table 4-1) are not enough to help them maintain their marriage(s). What I think happens is that as soon as the marriage vows are spoken, each partner ceases to exist as a person and their role as husband or wife becomes their spouse's primary concern. From my professional observation, it seems that African-Americans consciously or unconsciously develops their ideas about marital roles through (1) observation and imitation of their parent(s), (2) observation and imitation of other parents that they hold in high regard, (3) religious doctrine and (4) television family sitcoms and/or other media. The problem with all of this is that neither spouse communicates their ideas to the other. Once the marriage starts, whenever a spouse unwittingly violates a tenet of their role, they are held accountable for the violation and resentment is developed. The top 9 ideas of African-Americans about the marital roles that their spouse *should* fulfill, are in Table 5-1.

TABLE 5-1
What should be your *Special Friend's* role in marriage?

Single African-American Women *(Husband's Role)*

Ages 22-28	Ages 29-36	Ages 37-43
1) Have a job	1) Friend	1) Have a job
2) Friend	2) Have a Job	2) Emotional Support
3) Emotional Support	3) Emotional Support	3) Friend
4) Only Sexual Partner	4) Only Sexual Partner	4) Only Sexual Partner
5) Child Care	5) Child Care	5) Cleaning
6) Cleaning	6) Cleaning	6) Cooking
7) Cooking	7) - Cooking - Final Decision Maker	7) Child Care
8) Final Decision Maker	8) Handle the Money	8) Handle the Money
9) Handle the Money	9) ————	9) Final Decision Maker

Single African-American Men *(Wife's Role)*

Ages 22-28	Ages 29-36	Ages 37-43
1) Friend	1) Friend	1) Friend
2) Emotional Support	2) Emotional Support	2) Emotional Support
3) Have a Job	3) Have a Job	3) Have a Job
4) Child Care	4) Only Sexual Partner	4) Child Care
5) Cooking	5) Child Care	5) Cooking

TABLE 5-1 (Contd.)

6) Cleaning	6) Cooking	6) Only Sexual Partner
7) Only Sexual Partner	7) Cleaning	7) Cleaning
8) Handle the Money	8) Handle the Money	8) Handle the Money
9) Final Decision Maker	9) Final Decision Maker	9) Final Decision Maker

The Language of Conflict

As couples go through the mating/marital process, gender differences and life's pressures start to create situations where individual wants/needs (*mainly wants*) are not met and resentments are created. As wants/needs continue not to be met, resentments become problems and then conflicts because nobody knows how to get their own wants/needs met, when their own wants/needs are not being met. Then depending on how the relationship is viewed as progressing and the desire to get wants/needs met, either partner will try to let the other partner know that there is a problem. The top 6 ways that each partner could let their partner know that there is a problem, see Table 5-2.

TABLE 5-2
How do you let your *Special Friend* know that there is a problem in the relationship?

Single African-American Women

<u>Ages 22-28</u>	<u>Ages 29-36</u>	<u>Ages 37-43</u>
1) Tell him	1) Tell him	1) Tell him
2) By staying away for a while	2) By staying away for a while	2) By staying away for a while

TABLE 5-2 (Contd.)

3) Complain	3) Complain	3) Stop talking
4) Stop being affectionate	4) Stop being affectionate	4) Complain
5) Stop talking	5) Stop talking	5) Stop being affectionate
6) Stop having sex	6) Stop having sex	6) Discuss it with his friend

Single African-American Men

Ages 22-28	Ages 29-36	Ages 37-43
1) Tell her	1) Tell her	1) Tell her
2) Complain	2) Complain	2) Complain
3) By staying away for a while	3) By staying away for a while	3) By staying away for a while
4) Discuss it with her friend	4) Discuss it with her friend	4) Stop talking
5) Stop talking	5) Stop talking	5) Stop being affectionate
6) Stop being affectionate	6) Stop being affectionate	6) Discuss it with her friend

As indicated in Table 5-2, it seems that both African-American men and women try to let their partner know that there is a problem by talking to them. This talking is seen as communication, however, it is my contention that in the majority of intimate relationships, communication has not really taken place. This is not because of a lack of effort but because of a lack of knowledge as to what constitutes true communication. This lack of knowledge about communication can be seen in the behavior of couples that come for counseling: (1) each are interrupting the other's comments, (2) sentences start with an attack "you" and/ or "you always" and (3) blaming each other for the present circumstance(s) of the relationship.

What usually happens in intimate relationships is that men and women *talk to* or *talk at* each other. This means that when someone (the speaker) begins to talk, as the other person (the listener) begins to hear what is being said, the listener's concern about what he or she *thinks* is being said, comes into his or her mind. The listener then wants to express his or her thoughts about what they think is being said and interrupts the speaker, in an effort to get their concerns heard. The speaker upon being interrupted, becomes agitated and begins to reiterate their thoughts and increases their vocal level to indicate that they want to be heard. The listener then feels that they have not been heard, becomes agitated and in a raised vocal level, begins again to interrupt the speaker. This cycle continues until someone breaks off the talking or a physical confrontation takes place. This is *the language of conflict*, see Figure 5-1. When you use the language of conflict, you cannot resolve problems because you do not hear what the other person's wants and/or needs are, you only hear what is *your own* wants/needs.

This lack of knowledge about communication, is one of the major causes of conflict within intimate relationship(s). Without communication, the intimate relationship has little chance of success.

Figure 5-1
The Language of
Conflict

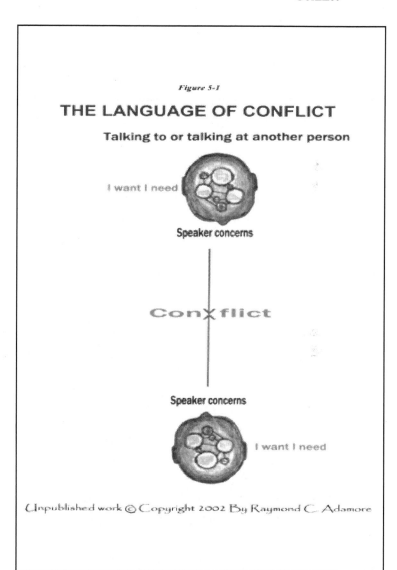

The Role of Anger

All of the following information in this book, on anger and rage, is the result of the practical application of a cyclic model of anger, gleaned from Jerry Medol, group leader of the Kansas City Men's Group.

When there are unresolved wants/needs (*mainly wants*) in intimate relationships, resentments give way to anger. When we talk about anger, we are talking about an *emotion* that all human beings are born with, regardless of race or gender. Anger is an emotion that we have to help us survive a *Threat,* which in the past was usually an animal. In today's society, with basically few animals to fear, anger has become our defense against threats presented by human beings. In *The Third Side: Why We Fight and How We Can Stop,* author William Ury states that in the first 99% of human history, because of a need to cooperation, there is little or no evidence found of conflict between human beings. However, within the last 1% of human history (the last five thousand years), with the advent of agriculture, the incidence of conflict between human beings has escalated.

Threats by human beings takes on two forms: (1) real or (2) psychological. A *real* threat can be (1) gun to the head, (2) a beating or (3) being raped. A *psychological* threat can be (1) jealousy, (2) control issues or (3) the breakup of a mating/ marital relationship(s).

Because there are so many threatening things that can happen to us within our environment, instead of trying to name them all, we will just call these threatening happenings an *Event.* If we perceive a threat (real/psychological) within an event, there are physical and emotional preparations that our body makes in order to help us fight or flee that threat. These physical and emotional preparations are called *Body Signs.*

66

Since human beings have different body makeups, some of the possible physical preparations that might take place are (1) an increase in heart rate and blood pressure, (2) there may be a rush of adrenalin, (3) a tenseness in the body and/or (4) a clenching of the fist.

Some of the possible emotional preparations that might take place are (1) a feeling of impatience, (2) a feeling of frustration, (3) a feeling of indifference and/or (4) a feeling of fear.

Once the body signs have kicked in, we then begin to feel angry. *Feeling angry is okay.* There is nothing wrong with feeling angry. The feeling of anger is telling you something about the event. Anger is telling you one of two things about the event, either (1) *what is happening is not what you want/need* or (2) *what you want/need is not happening.*

Either through socialization or life experience, we have learned not to react immediately to our anger, instead we *repress* it. In order for us to repress our anger, we must use some of our *body energy to* turn the energy of anger *inwards* upon ourselves. The energy from repressed anger that has been turned inwards upon ourselves, at some point in time, begins to affect the body. There are several medical illnesses that have been identified, that is initiated or maintained by repressed anger. These medical illnesses are (1) high blood pressure, (2) strokes, (3) heart attacks, (4) depression, (5) diabetes, (6) headaches, (7) weight gain/loss, (8) skin problems, (9) ulcers and (10) abuse of alcohol and/or drugs. These are medical illnesses that are rampant in the African-American community (See Figure 5-2).

Again, feeling angry is okay; however, once we repress our anger, we start to engage in behaviors listed in Table 5-2, which according to author Jo Clancy, in *Anger and Addiction: Breaking the Relapse Cycle*, would be considered as passive-explosive behaviors which leads to resentments.

Figure 5-2
Repressed Anger

The Introduction of Violence

Repressed anger has an accumulative effect. The more anger we repress, the more body energy we need to keep that anger repressed. Repressed anger that we allow to fester begins to change into a feeling of *rage* and then rage builds up within us. At some point in time, when a threatening event happens, either there might not be enough body energy left or there is no desire to repress the anger, we then react to our rage and violent/ abusive behavior erupts. When we react to our rage, we are no longer into *feelings,* we are now into *behavior.*

A person who is raging and has not given any previous indication that they were angry, the violent/abusive behavior seems to come out of nowhere. When we are harmed by the violent behavior of someone whom we love and who says that they love us; we have an issue with accepting that behavior. "How can someone love me and do this to me?" Let me try and explain this by talking a little about the feeling of *indifference.* Remember, indifference is part of the body signs (emotional preparation) that help us fight or flee a threat (real/ psychological). When we think of love, we think about *caring.* Indifference on the other hand is about *not caring* at all. Therefore, when a human being is feeling indifferent, he or she can do anything, anywhere, at anytime, to anybody or thing; because at that time, they do not care. Love has nothing to do with it.

In the majority of cases, the violent/abusive behavior that is taking place is not only based on the rage from the immediate situation but also from part or all of the stored up rage within them. The resulting violence can become quite brutal (i.e., mutilations, multiple wounds, multiple killings, etc.).

Drama and the Search for Mr./Mrs. Right:
Understanding the Cycle of Mistreatment

When a person is raging and erupts in *violent* behavior: (1) bruises are put on people's bodies, (2) people are placed in hospitals, (3) people die and (4) property is destroyed. Society becomes aware of the violent behavior (*not the abusive behavior*) in intimate relationships because of hospital and police records. When this happens, society punishes the person, mostly men, with jail time. Once society has acted, it is felt that violence has been dealt with; then comes the next time.

In comparison, when a person is raging and erupts in *abusive* (verbal and/or attitudinal) behavior, they are committing a psychological attack upon another human being. Psychological attacks such as gossiping, humiliating and bullying, leave no signs of physical violence, however, they affect the human psyche. The recipient of these attacks may later exhibit behaviors that are destructive to themselves and/or others.

In the African-American community, the African-American woman's verbal and attitudinal rage is well known, as indicated by author Shahrazad Ali, in *The Blackman's Guide to Understanding the Blackwoman.* When there is an intent to harm, the African-American woman's verbal and attitudinal rage becomes abusive. There are three things an African-American woman can say to an African-American man that will cause him mental aghast. They are (1) to belittle his financial ability, (2) to belittle his sexual ability and/or (3) to belittle some woman that he holds in high regard. In most cases, the African-American man's mental aghast is followed by a physical attack upon the African-American woman.

When you are having a raging incident, the functionality of the immune system is decreased for up to *six hours*. Also, when you have a raging incident, there will *always* be some residual rage left over and it takes about *two- hours* for your body to return to a calm state. Therefore, within that two-hour time frame, you need to do something that will help you calm down (e.g., listen to music, cook, talk on the phone, play hoops, go for a walk, etc.) or try to devise a way to change the negative energy of rage into something positive (i.e., stop smoking or create an organization to fight the injustice). What you do not want to do, is to continue to rehash that event, over and over again in your mind, because this will only keep you raging and then erupting into violent/abusive behavior. You also do not want to (1) be near a gun or knife, (2) get behind the wheel of a car or (3) ride a motorcycle, because these can become weapons and you can either hurt or kill yourself or someone else. If in that two-hour time frame, another event triggers your rage, you will still need two hours from the last triggering event to calm down. Consequently, it is quite possible for a person to be in a rage all day long because they have not had enough time to calm down.

Although anger is a human emotion, the acting out of violent/abusive behavior is based on learned behavior. In the majority of cases, when a male becomes angry, he will become violent (physical) and when a female becomes angry, she will become abusive (verbal and/or attitudinal). This does not mean that the behaviors are not interchangeable, men being abusive and women being violent, however, in general the gender behaviors are as stated.

When a human being is displaying violent/abusive behavior, what that person is trying to do, is to get his or her wants/needs met by force or intimidation. At the time of the violent/abusive behavior, he or she is into *power* and *control*. Power and control is not a male issue. It is a *human* issue. The violent/abusive individual is trying to have power and control over the individual(s) or the situation. In reality, you may have some influence over another individual or the situation, but you do not have power and control. You can only have power and control over *yourself,*

71

however, most of us are trying to have power and control over others (our partners) and not over ourselves.

Once an event has taken place and we perceive that event as threatening (real/psychological), the body signs kick in, we feel angry, we rage and then we react by becoming violent or abusive; the *Cycle of Rage* has been created and it is self-perpetuating. (See Figure 5-3) All of this takes place quicker than it takes for you to snap your fingers.

Figure 5-3
Reaction to Rage

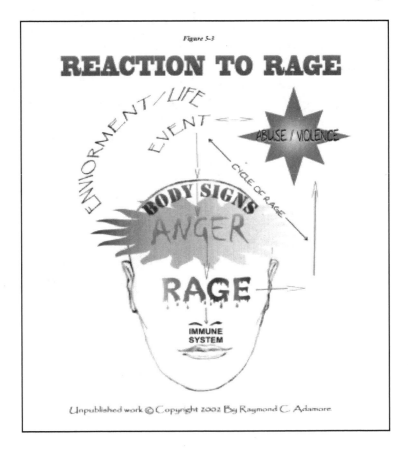

Once the Cycle of Rage has been created, anytime an event takes place which seems similar to a previous event that we perceived as threatening, we do not have to go through the Cycle of Rage again; we will go directly to the behavior (violent/abusive) that we did then or wanted to do, but was not able to do at the time. Therefore, if we were violent or wanted to be violent in dealing with the initial event, we will automatically be violent in dealing with a perceived similar event. Also, we would automatically be abusive when we find ourselves confronted with a perceived similar event, where in the initial event, we were abusive or wanted to be abusive. An example of this can be seen in most *domestic violence* situations.

Domestic violence does not start when a man hits a woman. It starts during the childhood of the man. During this time, if the man child sees his mother being *inappropriate* (violent/abusive) with his father and if the man child feels that the mother is *unjustly* using violent and/or abusive behavior on him; he will tolerate this because (1) he wants to please his mother and (2) at this point in his development, the mother is physically stronger than he is and can force her will on him. As this violent and/or abusive behavior continues, he makes a conscious decision that he is not going to let another woman treat him this way. This decision is then repressed and sent into the unconscious mind.

Now as an adult, when he feels that he has developed to the point where he can defend himself; when he feels that his partner/spouse is unjustly attacking him with violent/abusive behavior, his unconscious rage is triggered. It seems to him that he is in the same unjust situation that he was in with his mother and because he had decided that he would not let another woman treat him that way; now that he can defend himself, he reacts to his rage and erupts with violent/abusive behavior. All of this happens without conscious thought. Depending on his rage at that particular situation and the degree of repressed rage that also erupts, the reaction can be quite brutal. And once that he has reacted to his rage, whenever he feels threaten in a similar manner, he will erupt again.

One of the things that a man might do to avoid attacking the woman is to exit the conflict situation, however, if his exit is blocked by the woman because she "has to be heard," then the attack will take place. Other efforts such as (1) hitting the wall with his fist or (2) throwing something at the wall, are seen as threatening or intimidating by women.

Once the raging incident is over and the man has had time to calm down, he may become remorseful and try to *smooth over* the incident. Now would be a good time for both partners to seek counseling in an effort to get at the conscious and/or unconscious cause(s) of the rage and try to minimize further incidents. In domestic violence cases, the counseling option has not been given serious consideration because of the violent attacks. However, in the majority of cases, I believe that research in this area will show that counseling can be affective in reducing the incidence of attacks.

At this point, I hope that I have been able to explain the *genesis of conflict* and show the typical behavior of human beings who are involved in conflict within their intimate relationship(s). Ways to reduce conflict within intimate relationships are discussed in Chapter 6.

Chapter 6

New Directions

A holistic evaluation of African-American mating/marital behavior cannot be done without taking into consideration the total history of the African-Americans. This lack of consideration does not take into account their African history and the impact of American slavery on their psychological and social mind set. I contend that this lack of a holistic approach has helped contribute to the high divorce rate and turmoil in African-American mating/ marital relationships, however, we have the ability to turn this around. We need to go in some *new directions.*

Now that we have looked into the mirror and seen our reflection, there still seems to be some blemishes that we cannot cover up with denial. One of those blemishes seems to be that neither African-American men nor women have taken the time to determine what their own wants/needs are. Their wants/needs seem to be based on all kinds of information from various outside sources such as parents, peers, religion and the media. They have not taken the time to sort out the good information from the bad. Therefore, they seem to be functioning from a script and not from any self- knowledge.

Another blemish that I see is that African Americans seem to be rushing into the marital relationship based on the Hollywood version of mating and marriage. In the Hollywood version, men and women meet, become infatuated, have sex and then get married, all within about two hours. In today's reality, African-Americans seem to complete this process in less than twelve months and they are not taking the time to gain enough information or experience with their partners, to make as sound of a marriage decision as possible. The rationale for marriage seems to be based on the fact that they are having sex and things seem to be going good and that they need to take the next natural step: marriage, because that is the way the script is written. It seems that the time frames that I have indicated in this book, only become an afterthought when wants/needs (*mainly wants*) are not being met.

A third blemish seems to be that most African-American couples have not learned how to resolve mating/marital problems in a peaceful manner because they have only seen their parents resolve their differences by violent/abusive behavior. Parents should learn and teach their children that even if there are differences of opinion between partners, through compromise, one approach can be decided upon and if it is determined that it is not working, then the other approach is followed without blame.

And the final blemish is embedded in the lip service give to the African proverb: *It takes a community to raise a child.* No longer do African-American parents allow other adult African-Americans to correct the misconduct of their children. This is now seen as an interference to their parental rights and the respect for our elders, which is implied in this proverb, has been lost.

African Threads

One of the new directions is to reconnect with some ideas from our African culture. One of these ideas is the marital training of African-American child /children. I feel that this training should include having the male child/children participate in household responsibilities such as cleaning, cooking and child care. His participation in these responsibilities will help prepare him for family life. *We should raise our sons and daughters and not love our sons and raise our daughters.*

Also, there should be some training for both genders concerning household finances, credit and the maintenance of their own bank account. It has been my experience that both genders are more reluctant to share their financial habits than they are their sexual habits. The bill payment behavior and the way that the available money is budgeted, is usually an ongoing issue of contention. The degree to which this issue is handled in a timely manner, will determine the amount of conflict within the marriage.

In addition, there should also be some exchange of real information concerning sexuality and contraception.

Myths and Illusions

Another direction , is acknowledging some myths and illusions that African-Americans have embraced which I feel has no connection to real human behavior and has a negative impact on their present day intimate relationships.

Let's look at the illusion and myth of *romance*. Romance is the idealization of everyday life. In intimate relationships, the woman expects that the man will engage in behavior that is in total deference to her wishes throughout their intimate relationship. Although this type of behavior can be carried on for long periods of time, it may not be carried on forever. When the man does not continue this behavior, she places the intimate relationship into turmoil. Therefore, making life decisions about marriage based on just romantic illusions, is asking for trouble. We need to stop fantasizing so much about romance in our intimate relationships and start dealing with real human behavior.

Drama and the Search for Mr./Mrs. Right:
Understanding the Cycle of Mistreatment

One of the major religious and romantic myths is the idea concerning the natural order of human sexuality. There are some realities that need to be brought to the forefront in the discussion of the natural order of human sexuality: (1) that human beings are mammals and that only 2% of this planet's mammals are sexually monogamous, (2) in accordance with authors Christopher Ryan and Cacilda Jetha', in *Sex At Dawn*, the natural order of human sexuality is *promiscuity* not monogamy, (3) that *sexual monogamy is a choice* and (4) with the *demand* for sexual monogamous behavior in marital relationships, there is a denial and/or avoidance of real human sexual behavior which could lead to emotional disappointment, sexual infidelity and/or *sexual boredom* (repeated mundane sexual activity with the same person).

Another major religious and romantic illusion is that marriages will last "til death do us part." We do not look at marital relationships as life experiences that have varied beginnings and endings. According to Dr. Helen Fisher, on the Discovery Channel program, *Science of Sex Appeal*, seen on November 13, 2010, that breakups in marriages usually happen after four and some half years of marriage and the majority of divorces are usually initiated by women. With African-American marriages experiencing a high rate of divorce and turmoil in the majority of those that remain intact, the idea of "til death do us part" is not a reality for the majority of African-American marriages.

There is also a myth that money solves everything. In an interview of the billionaire businessman Ted Turner, by Charlie Rose, host of the *Charlie Rose Show*, shortly after Ted Turner had lost a huge sum of money in the stock market and who had been recently divorced from Jane Fonda; Charlie Rose asked Ted Turner what was his biggest regret? Ted Turner's reply: "That I was not better in my personal relationships."

The Language of Cooperation

In Table 6-1, we see the top 5 ways African-Americans try to resolve conflict within their intimate relationships and the importance of communication.

In my years of counseling intimate couples, the Language of Conflict was a common phenomenon. In an effort to bring about a different way of communicating, the *Language of Cooperation,* was introduced as a means to help reduce the incidence of conflict within intimate relationships.

TABLE 6-1

How do you try to solve a problem that comes up in the relationship with your *Special Friend?*

Single African-American Women

Ages 22-28	Ages 29-36	Ages 37-43
1) Discuss it with him	1) Discuss it with him	1) Discuss it with him
2) Compromise	2) Compromise	2) Compromise
3) Seek advice from an outside source	3) Seek advice from an outside source	3) Agree to disagree
4) Agree to disagree	4) Arguing	4) Seek advice from an outside source
5) Arguing	5) Agree to disagree	5) ———

TABLE 6-1 (Contd.)

Single African-American Men

<u>Ages 22-28</u>	<u>Ages 29-36</u>	<u>Ages 37-43</u>
1) Discuss it with her	1) Discuss it with her	1) Discuss it with her
2) Compromise	2) Compromise	2) Compromise
3) Seek advice from an outside source	3) Seek advice from an outside source	3) Agree to disagree
4) Agree to disagree	4) Agree to disagree	4) Arguing
5) Arguing	5) Give in	5) Avoid discussing it

When we use the language of cooperation, talking is involved, however, it is not the main function; *listening* is the main function. When using the language of cooperation, it makes no difference who starts to talk. When someone starts to talk, it is automatically the other persons responsibility to listen.

In order to learn how to listen, the listener *must* understand that once he or she begins to hear what the speaker is saying and the listener's concerns about what he or she thinks is being said, comes into his or her mind, at this point, the listener's concerns are *not* important. The listener's concerns about what he or she thinks is being said, *must* be put on the "back burner" (i.e., mental/ verbal hold). Only in this way can the listener really *hear* what the speaker is trying to say to him or her.

Once the listener is listening, there should be only four reasons why the listener should interrupt the speaker. The first reason to interrupt, is when the listener wants to *postpone* the communication to another time. There is nothing wrong with the listener postponing the communication to another time. The listener may be (1) tired, (2) they may have heard it before and do not now want to hear it again, (3) they might be overwhelmed by other things at the moment and cannot handle anything else or (4) they might not be feeling well. However, postponing the communication to another time, is not getting the listener out of anything. When the listener postpones the communication to another time (e.g., tomorrow at 8:00 p.m.), the listener must be there, at the appointed time, ready to listen to whatever the speaker has to say. If this is not done, the listener is being disrespectful of the speaker and disrespect is not a part of good communication.

The second reason to interrupt, is when the listener needs *clarification* about some detail that the speaker is talking about at the moment. This is not the same as the listener's concerns at the beginning of the discourse. The listener's concerns are still on the "back burner."

A third reason to interrupt the speaker would be when he or she starts to *repeat themselves* because since you have been listening to the speaker, there should be no reason for him or her to repeat themselves.

Finally, the fourth reason to interrupt is when he or she starts to *jump from subject to subject* because in order for the participants to come to some resolution of an issue or situation, it is important to complete one subject at a time before moving on to the next issue or situation.

If there is no reason to interrupt the speaker, then the listener should listen until the speaker has run the length of their thought processes concerning the subject which they are talking about. If it takes them an hour, give them that hour. When the speaker has finished, the listener needs to give the speaker *feedback* as to what they heard. This feedback is necessary and important because the listener might have misinterpreted something that the speaker has said, thereby, creating a misunderstanding about what the speaker was talking about. If there is any misunderstanding, the speaker should give the listener further clarification. This exchange is part of the feedback process and the listener should let this process take place.

When the feedback process is over and the listener now knows what was being said to him or her, now is the time for the listener to determine if their concerns, which has been on the "back burner" all this time, now needs to be expressed to the speaker. If so, the listener becomes the speaker, the speaker now becomes the listener and the communication process starts all over again. The new listener, should not interrupt the new speaker for any reason other than for the four reasons that I have previously mentioned (1) postponement, (2) clarification, (3) repeating themselves and/or (4) jumping from subject to subject. (See Figure 6-1)

Using the language of cooperation is a circular process. Someone speaks and the other person listens. Feedback is given. And then, the listener becomes the speaker, the speaker becomes the listener and feedback is given. When using the language of cooperation, you can *always* tell when the listener was not listening, because any response that he or she gives you, will have nothing to do with the subject matter that you were talking about.

The reason for the language of cooperation goes back to my premise about human being's wants/needs. Because people are trying to get their own wants/needs met, this is what they are talking about most of the time. All you have to do is to listen to them and they will tell you what they want/need. In intimate relationships, it is each partner's main responsibility to meet their partner's wants/needs, not just their own. By listening, you will become aware of your partner's wants/needs and you can either (1) meet their want/needs immediately, (2) meet them at another time or (3) give your partner a reason why you cannot meet them at all.

Figure 6-1
The Language of
Cooperation

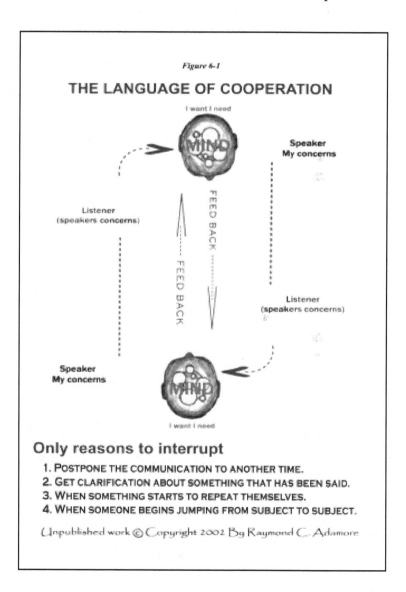

Figure 6-1

THE LANGUAGE OF COOPERATION

I want I need

Speaker
My concerns

FEED BACK

Listener
(speakers concerns)

FEED BACK

Listener
(speakers concerns)

Speaker
My concerns

I want I need

Only reasons to interrupt
1. POSTPONE THE COMMUNICATION TO ANOTHER TIME.
2. GET CLARIFICATION ABOUT SOMETHING THAT HAS BEEN SAID.
3. WHEN SOMETHING STARTS TO REPEAT THEMSELVES.
4. WHEN SOMEONE BEGINS JUMPING FROM SUBJECT TO SUBJECT.

Drama and the Search for Mr./Mrs. Right:
Understanding the Cycle of Mistreatment

In my counseling practice, although I found it easy to explain to my clients the mechanics of the language of cooperation, they found that it was the hardest thing for them to do. This was because both genders resisted putting their concerns on the "back burner," when their partner was hurling accusations at them. They felt that they had to defend themselves. However, if the listener can resist the need to defend themselves (not taking personally any negative statements that is being said to them at the time) and keeps their concerns on the "back burner" until a later time, then the language of cooperation can be effective.

In addition, because my clients were having a problem with practicing the language of cooperation, they also had a problem with achieving a *compromise*. In order to achieve a compromise, there needs to be a further understanding of listening. Listening, as a major part of communication, is not only important because it will help you to determine the wants/needs of another human being; it will also help you to arrive at a compromise, when there is a disagreement concerning the wants/needs of an issue. When there is a disagreement as to the wants/needs of an issue, what usually happens is that each partner tries to change their partner's wants/needs to that of their own, thereby creating resistance and anger. A better solution is for *each partner* to look at their own wants/needs concerning an issue of disagreement, knowing what their partner's wants/needs are concerning that issue because they have been listening to their partner; then *each partner* needs to determine how they can change their own wants/needs to a position that is closer to their partner's wants/needs, without losing their sense of whom they are. *This is how you arrive at a compromise.*

If in a good faith effort, a compromise on an issue cannot be obtained, then an agreement to disagree is appropriate. Differences of opinion are just that, differences of opinion. Because a person has a different opinion, does not make them an enemy. Problems arise when a person(s) tries to *force* their opinion onto others.

Reduction of Violence

Another directional change for intimate couples is learning how to control their anger. When human beings feel threaten, become enraged and then want to act on their rage, they will engage in violent/abusive behavior. It is obvious from the information presented, that this form of behavior is destructive to us and others. Another way to deal with our rage is to learn how to *Respond* to anger. In order to respond to anger, a human being has to stop acting on emotions and begin to *think*.

The first step in learning how to respond to anger is to know than anger is more than an emotion that we are born with and that it exists for our survival. We need to know that anger is a *secondary emotion*. A secondary emotion, is an emotion that has to be triggered by another emotion before it becomes active. In an event that we perceive as threatening, one or any combination of five emotions *must* be triggered, before we will become angry. These five emotions are *hurt, loss, pain, frustration* and *fear*, and they are called the *Triggers to Anger*.

Of the triggers to anger, human anger is mostly triggered by the emotions of *frustration* and/or *fear*. Human beings become frustrated when their wants/needs *(mainly wants)* are being blocked. Human beings are not only fearful of other human beings and the unknown, but, they are also afraid that a negative event that has already taken place, will happen again.

Also, *nobody* can make you angry. Anger is an emotion that is inside you and it is your reaction to a perceived threatening event. We are each responsible for our own anger. However, although nobody can make you angry, human beings can *act* in such a way as to trigger: hurt, loss, pain, frustration and/or fear within us and we can also *act* in such a way that we will trigger: hurt, loss, pain, frustration and/or fear within them. *This is how anger works*.

Secondly, as you have been reading this book, your eyes have been blinking and you have not given it any thought. The blinking of your eyes is an automatic function of your body. If you think only about your eyes not blinking, they will not blink. However, once another thought comes into your mind, the automatic functioning of your body will take over and your eyes will blink. This exercise verifies that the mind *can* control the body. In the same manner, every time you have had an anger episode, your body signs have been activated, to prepare you to fight or flee the threat and you have not been paying any attention to them. You need to start paying attention to your own body signs which are activated when you are in an angry situation (e.g., clutched fist, increased heart rate, a feeling of impatience, a feeling of frustration, etc.) and *know them.* The importance of knowing your own body signs is that they are activated, just before you start to feel the feeling of anger. (Again, feeling angry is okay. Anger is telling you something about the event, either (1) what is happening is not what you want/need or (2) what you want/need is not happening). Therefore, your body signs are a warning that you are becoming angry.

Once you have learned your body signs and the triggers to anger, based on this information, while you are in a calm state, you need to make a conscious decision, that when you perceive an event as threatening, unless the threat is real (e.g., a knife to your throat, a beating, being raped, etc.), you are not going to engage in any violent/abusive behavior. When you are in a life-threatening situation, you *must* take action that you feel will insure your survival, however, the majority of our lives are not involved in any life-threatening situations. We just act as if every threatening event is life-threatening.

The next thing that you need to do is to *Back-Off* from the feeling of anger by either physically or mentally removing yourself from the anger situation. We all know how to physically remove ourselves from an anger situation, however, how do you mentally remove yourself? You can mentally remove yourself from an anger situation by not taking personally, *any* negative statements that are being said to you at the time because once you do, you will begin to rage and then react with violent/abusive behavior.

The purpose of backing-off is to determine what your *Options* are. You need to take the time to think about what emotion(s) triggered this anger episode for *you* (hurt, loss, pain, frustration, and/or fear) and what do you want and/or need to happen in this situation to change the event into a more positive situation for yourself.

Once you have determined what your options are, you need to *communicate* your wants/needs to the other person and leave it alone. (See Figure 6-2.) You are not going to try to force anyone to meet your wants/needs by being violent and/or abusive. When you have communicated your wants/needs, people will meet your wants/needs or they will not. There are no half measures.

When you have communicated your wants/needs and they are not being met, instead of erupting into violent/abusive behavior, you need to *make a decision*. There are four possible decisions that you can make. These decisions are (1) is there another way to get my wants/needs met, instead of the way I am trying to get them met, (2) is it important that I get my wants/needs met at this particular point in time, (3) is it important that this person has to meet my wants/needs at all; because you may be asking the person to do something that they do not have the capacity to do and (4) if my wants/needs are not being met over a long period of time, why am I still in this relationship? Every time you have had an anger episode, you needed to make one of these four decisions and you did not.

Figure 6-2
Response to Anger

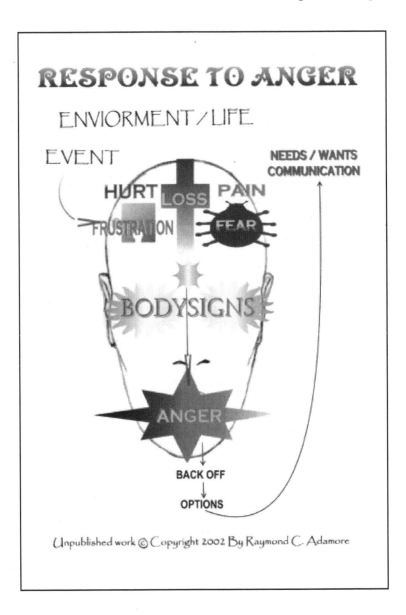

Counseling Assistance

Another new direction can be gleaned from Table 6-1. It seems that both single African-American men and women are willing to seek advice from an outside source, in an effort to resolve conflict within their intimate relationships. For the African-American, this means going to a friend or a minister. Although these sources may be helpful, I would highly recommend that professional counseling be given a try. Although more African-Americans are seeking counseling, the problems of (1) cost, (2) that they do not want to air their "dirty laundry" in front of a stranger, (3) they do not want anyone telling them what to do and (4) the refusal of African-American women to accept any responsibility for problems within their intimate relationship, are the main reasons why the majority of African-Americans are not getting the professional help that they need.

However, when counseling is sought, it has been my experience that about 55% of African-American women and about 45% of African-American men will make the initial contact. About 50% of the contacts were made during what Lenore E. Walker, in *The Battered Woman*, termed the third phase of the Cycle Theory of Violence; where the offender uses kindness and loving behavior, after some violence has taken place.

Although there is an increasing amount of awareness of domestic violence incidences, there does not seem to be anything that has been effectively done to decrease its occurrence. There seems to be a school of thought that jail is the only answer for the offender and that counseling does not help reduce the continued increase in domestic violence. It has been my experience that by providing both parties with the educational information about (1) communication (e.g., the language of conflict and the language of cooperation), (2) the genesis of conflict (e.g., wants/needs, anger and rage) and (3) using cognitive-behavior therapy to deal with the underlining issues that the partners/spouses are bringing to the relationship, there can be a decrease in the incidence of violent/ abusive behavior within the intimate relationship.

Conflict within intimate relationships is an universal occurrence. It does not discriminates because of race, gender, sexual orientation, economic and educational status, etc. It is my contention that conflict takes place within intimate relationships because human beings bring their unresolved wants/needs (*mainly wants*) into the relationship and are looking for their partner/spouse to resolve or help resolve them. This may be conscious or unconscious to the human beings that are involved in the intimate relationship.

Once a person has battered, if the perceived threatening elements continue, they will batter again. This is why I recommend that counseling be sought during the kindness and loving stage after the onslaught of a violent/abusive outbreak because I feel that this is a way to break the cycle of violent/abusive behavior. Because of the innate nature of anger within human beings, it seems that the best outcome that can be expected is a decrease in violent/ abusive behavior as opposed to its elimination.

As descendants of African slaves, we African-Americans take pride in the factor that we have survived American slavery, however, at what cost? We know more about the history and philosophy of our kidnappers than we know about ourselves. Because of the implications of *Integration* (e.g., lost of African-American economic development) and the disconnect from our African culture, we see ourselves and other Africans through the prism of our kidnappers. This has further distanced us from our African brothers and sisters. We have forgotten the principles of our African-American great grandparents, *education and hard work*. Because a few of us have gotten through the net of miseducation, unemployment and underemployment, we feel comfortable. However, if we African-Americans continue on the path that we are on, we may not survive into the future. We need to regain our principles, history and philosophy and begin to live instead of just survive. We are a strong and intelligent people and are capable of solving our own problems. I hope that the information that I have laid out in this book, will be helpful to African-American men and women as they persuade Mr./Ms. Right. The only thing that is needed now is the *will* to change.

Let me leave you with these final thoughts. There is a combination of positive and negative energy within the Universe, the same as it is within human beings. It seems easier for human beings to focus on the negative energy than on the positive energy. When human beings focus on negative energy, they can only see a negative Universe. However, when human beings focus on positive energy, they can see both a positive and negative Universe and act accordingly.

Appendix A

Adamore's Relationship Questionnaire
Form A (Unmarried)

DATE: _____ AGE: _____ SEX (Circle)   M   F

RELIGIOUS BACKGROUND _____

EDUCATION COMPLETED (Circle):

      10 11 12 13 14 15 B M PhD

MARITAL STATUS:

      SINGLE _____
      SEPARATED _____
      WIDOWED _____
      DIVORCED _____
      LIVING WITH SEXUAL PARTNER _____

NUMBER OF CHILDREN _____

ANNUAL INCOME _____

ETHNIC BACKGROUND:

      AFRICAN-AMERICAN _____
      HISPANIC _____
      CAUCASIAN _____
      ORIENTAL _____
      OTHER _____

DIRECTIONS

This study is being attempted to determine attitudes, values and practices of the African-American (Blacks) premarital relationships. Major research on this subject such as the <u>Kinsey Report</u> and the <u>Hite Report</u> contains little or no data pertaining directly to the relationships of African-Americans, Hispanics or other minorities. However, by your voluntary participation in this study, you can assist me in correcting this over sight. This information will be used to create a book, articles, and for other media activities.

<u>The content of this questionnaire deals with social arrangements between members of the</u> **OPPOSITE SEX** which lead to a very personal and intimate relationship. Other types of relationships may or may not involve sexual activity. **THIS IS NOT A TEST.** Please read the following questions **CAREFULLY.** These questions are dealing with sexual subjects such as: intercourse, physical aspects of the human body, oral sex, abortion and contraception. Because this questionnaire does not ask for your name, your identity and the confidentiality of your responses will remain anonymous. There are no wrong or right answers. It is expected that you will answer the questions that are asked, regardless of your own particular sex. If you have any questions, please ask for assistance. Your cooperation is appreciated. **THANK YOU.**

Drama and the Search for Mr./Mrs. Right:
Understanding the Cycle of Mistreatment

1. Where would you go to meet someone of the opposite sex? Please rank the following in the order of your preferences with 1 being the highest, 2 the second highest, and so on, with 11 being the lowest ranking.

_____ Cultural Event _____ Lounge _____ Work

_____ School _____ Church _____ Recreational Event

_____ Party _____ Through Friend _____ Supermarket

_____ Shopping Center (Mall) _____ Other (tell what) _____

2. Do you make the first move in and effort to start a relationship?

_____ Yes _____ No

Please explain: _____
_____
_____

3. After the first meeting, what is it about a member of the opposite sex, that you will take into consideration for continuing the relationship? Please rank the following in the order of your preferences, with 1 being the highest, 2 the second highest, and so on, with 8 being the lowest ranking.

_____ Education   _____ Sexual attraction

_____ Physical appearance _____ Sensibility (Vibes)

_____ Job   _____ Religion

_____ Car   _____ Other (tell what)

                          _____

4. What is it about the physical appearance of someone of the opposite sex that gets your attention? Please rank the following in the order of your preferences, with 1 being the highest, 2 the second highest, and so on, with 11 being the lowest ranking.

_____ Eyes   _____ Skin Color   _____ Hair

_____ Legs   _____ Breast/Chest   _____ Genital Area

_____ Hands   _____ Buttock   _____ Other (tell what)

                                    _____

_____ Smile   _____ Feet

5. What types of physical contact do you want on the first date? Please rank the following in the order of your preferences, with 1 being the highest, 2 the second highest, and so on, with 7 being the lowest ranking.

_____ Kiss   _____ Casual touching

_____ Have Sex   _____ Hug

_____ Pet   _____ Other (tell what)

                        _____

_____ Hold Hands

6. How much time should pass before the female should offer to share of pay the expenses for an evening out on the town?

_____ On the first date _____ 3-4 months _____ 9-10 months

_____ 1-3 weeks _____ 5-6 months _____ 11 months or longer

_____ 1-2 months _____ 7-8 months _____ Never

A **SPECIAL FRIEND** IS SOMEONE OF THE OPPOSITE SEX THAT YOU ARE HAVING A RELATIONSHIP WITH WHICH INCLUDES SEXUAL ACTIVITY.

7. Are you presently involved in a relationship with a special friend which includes sexual activity?

_____ Yes _____ No

AN **INTIMATE RELATIONSHIP** IS DEFINED AS A VERY CLOSE RELATIONSHIP WHERE THERE IS A SHARING OF PERSONAL FEELINGS AND TRUST IS GIVEN.

8. Do you make the first attempt to start an intimate relationship?

_____ Yes _____ No

Please explain: _____

_____

_____

9. How much time passes before you become intimate in a relationship?

_____ Immediately _____ 3-4 months _____ 9-10 months

_____ 1-3 weeks _____ 5-6 months _____ 11 months or longer

_____ 1-2 months _____ 7-8 months

10. Do you try to initiate the first sexual contact?

_____ Yes _____ No

Please explain: _____

_____

_____

11. How much time passes before you become sexually active in a relationship?

_____ First meeting _____ 5-6 months

_____ 1-3 weeks _____ 7-8 months

_____ 1-2 months _____ 9-10 months

_____ 3-4 months _____ 11 months or longer

12. What are the sources of your information concerning sexual matters? Please rank your sources in the order of their importance, with 1 being the most important, 2 being the second importance, and so on, with 11 being the least important.

_____ School   _____ Movies

_____ Church   _____ Television

_____ Parents   _____ Friends

_____ Magazines/Book   _____ Experience

_____ Relatives   _____ Doctor

_____ Other (tell what)_____

13. Are you presently using any birth control methods or devices?

_____ Yes   _____ No

14. If you answered **NO** to question 13, what are your reasons for not using any birth control methods or devices? Please choose three (3) answers, with 1 being the first reason, 2 being the second reason and 3 being the third reason.

_____ Medical reasons   _____ To have children

_____ Religious reasons   _____ Limits sexual freedom

_____ Not satisfied with   _____ Sexual partner uses a
      choices of   method or device

birth control methods
or devices

_____ In love with sexual   _____ Not sexually active
           partner

_____ Other (tell what) _____

15. Would you engage in oral sex with your **SPECIAL FRIEND**?

_____ Yes   _____ No

16. What should a **SPECIAL** female do when she becomes pregnant? Please choose three (3) answers, with 1 being the first preference, 2 the second preference and 3 being the third preference.

_____ Get married, depending on   _____ Let relatives
           Special Friend   raise the child

_____ Give the baby up for adoption   _____ Have the child
                                                                         and raise it by
                                                                         herself

_____ Do not marry, but raise the child   _____ Give the child to
                                                                                 its father but
                                                                                 raise the child
                                                                                 with impact from
                                                                                 both parents

_____ Have an abortion   _____ Other (tell what)
                                                             _____

17. What should a **SPECIAL** male do when his **SPECIAL** female becomes pregnant? Please choose three (3) answers, with 1 being the first preference, 2 the second preference and 3 being the third preference.

_____ Get married, depending on Special Friend

_____ Let his relatives s raise the child

_____ Recommend giving the baby up adoption

_____ Do not marry, but share in the raising of the child

_____ Pay for an abortion

_____ If possible, raise the child by himself

_____ Do not marry, but provide financial support for the child

_____ Other (tell what)

_____

18. Does your parent's opinion of your **SPECIAL FRIEND** have any affect on your relationship with your **SPECIAL FRIEND**?

_____ Yes   _____ No

19. Does your friends opinion of your **SPECIAL FRIEND** have any affect on your relationship with your **SPECIAL FRIEND**?

_____ Yes   _____ No

20. Do you feel that your **SPECIAL FRIEND** should have a night out with their friends?

_____ Yes _____ No

21. Do you feel that your **SPECIAL FRIEND** should continue to have a close relationship with members of the opposite sex?

_____ Yes _____ No

Please explain: _____ _____
_____
_____

22. How much time should pass in the relationship before a **SPECIAL FRIEND** male should share or pay for a **SPECIAL FRIEND** female's financial obligations?

_____ Immediately _____ 5-6 months _____ After marriage/
living together

_____ 1-3 weeks _____ 7-8 months _____ Never

_____ 1-2 months _____ 9-10 months

_____ 3-4 months _____ 11 months or longer

Please explain: _____
_____
_____

23. Do you or your **SPECIAL FRIEND** have any children?

_____ Yes   _____ No

24. If you answered **Yes** to question 23, does the presence of the children have any affect on your relationship with your **SPECIAL FRIEND**?

_____ Yes   _____ No

Please explain: _____ _____

_____

_____

25. What should be a part of the relationship between you and your **SPECIAL FRIEND** that would help the relationship last over a long period of time? Please rank the following in the order of your preference with 1 being the highest, 2 the second highest, and so on, with 11 being the lowest ranking.

_____ Compatibility   _____ Sexual attraction

_____ Financial security   _____ Sharing of feelings

_____ Trust   _____ Respect

_____ Sense of Humor   _____ Friendship

_____ Emotional Support   _____ Other (tell what)

_____ Love   _____

26. In what ways do you let your **SPECIAL FRIEND** know that you care? Please rank the following in the order of your preferences with 1 being the highest, 2 the second highest, and so on, with 9 being the lowest ranking.

_____ Send greeting card   _____ Tell him/her

_____ Send flowers   _____ Have sex

_____ Provide Dinner (In/Out)   _____ Be affectionate,
without having
sex

_____ Buy gift   _____ Other (tell what)
        _____

_____ Give money

27. How do you let your **SPECIAL FRIEND** know that there is a problem in the relationship? Please choose three (3) answers, with 1 being the first method, 2 the second method and 3 being the third method.

_____ Tell him/her   _____ Complain

_____ Stop talking to him/her   _____ Stop having sex

_____ Stop being affectionate   _____ By staying away
for a while

_____ Have an affair   _____ Name calling/
Cursing

_____ Nag   _____ Other (tell what)

_____

_____ Discuss it with his/her friend

28. How do you try to solve a problem that comes up in the relationship with your **SPECIAL FRIEND**? Please choose three (3) answers, with 1 being the first method, 2 the second method and 3 being the third method.

_____ Discuss it with him/her   _____ Fighting

_____ Compromise   _____ Have an affair

_____ Ignore the problem   _____ Give in

_____ Have sex   _____ Avoid
                                              discussing it

_____ Arguing   _____ Agree to
                                              disagree

_____ Seek advice from an   _____ Other (tell what)
       outside source

29. Would you consider a live together arrangement as a possible result of the relationship with your **SPECIAL FRIEND**?

_____ Yes   _____ No

Please explain: _____

_____

_____

30. If you answered <u>YES</u> to question 29, how much time should pass after the relationship begins before you would enter into a live together arrangement?

_____ Less than a month   _____ 13-18 months

_____ 1-6 months   _____ 19-24 months

_____ 7-12 months   _____ More than 2
                                          years

31. Would you consider a live together arrangement as an alternative to marriage?

_____ Yes   _____ No

Please explain: _____

_____

_____

32. Would you consider marriage as a possible result of the relationship with your **SPECIAL FRIEND**?

_____ Yes   _____ No

Please explain: _____

_____

_____

33. If you answered <u>Yes</u> to question 32, how much time should pass after the relationship begins before you would enter into marriage?

_____ Less than a month   _____ 13-18 months

_____ 1-6 months   _____ 19-24 months

_____ 7-12 months   _____ More than 2
                                         years

34. What factors would you take into consideration in making a decision to marry? Please choose eight (8) answers and rank them with <u>1</u> being the first preference, <u>2</u> the second preference, and so on, with <u>8</u> being the eighth preference.

_____ Pregnancy   _____ Compatibility   _____ Education

_____ Love   _____ Trust   _____ Emotional
                                            Support

_____ Financial   _____ Desire to start   _____ Friendship
       security   a family

_____ Physical   _____ Companionship _____ Respect
       appearance

_____ Religion   _____ Personality   _____ Other (tell
                                            what)

                                                 _____

_____ Sexual   _____ Family
       attraction

35. What should be your **SPECIAL FRIEND'S** role in marriage? Please rank the following in the order of your preference with 1 being the highest, 2 the second highest, and so on, with 12 being the lowest ranking.

_____ Have a job   _____ Only sexual partner

_____ Child care   _____ Final decision maker

_____ Cleaning   _____ Emotional support

_____ Cooking   _____ Respectful

_____ Friend   _____ Handle the money

_____ Trustful   _____ Other (tell what)

_____

You have now reached the end of the questionnaire. Please check back to make sure that you have answered all of the questions as requested. Again, **THANK YOU** for your participation.

Appendix B

Methodology

The Adamore's Relationship Questionnaire (ARQ) was designed to (1) to determine the psychological, behavioral and motivational factors of individuals as they go through the mating/ marital process, (2) to provide a balanced gender perspective of intimate relationships and (3) provide a framework for the discussion of problems that impact intimate relationships,

The ARQ was administered to hundreds of Chicago State University (CSU) single African-American students, staff members, faculty members and other urban (Chicago) single African-Americans. The ARQ was administered directly to the participants either in the classrooms or one-on-one encounters and collected upon completion. Only 240 questionnaires were found to be useable for this book.

In discussions with faculty members from CSU's Math Department, it was determined that the minimum number of responses to a question that would make the responses statistically significant, would be thirty.

After trial and error, I finally determined that the age groupings used by Gould (1975) gave the best delineation of the data than any other age grouping.

Once I determined that I had the required number of useful questionnaires, the data was then compiled. The questionnaire contained two types of questions: (1) those that required the participant to rank their choices and (2) those that required a yes or no answer and a further explanation. For those questions that required the participant to rank their choices, a numerical value was give to each ranking (1=11 points; 2=10 points; 3=9 points;

4=8 points; 5=7 points; 6=6 points; 7=5 points; 8=4 points; 9=3 points; 10=2 points; 11=1 point and 0=0 point) and the numerical value of the total number of responses for each choice was totaled. Then the choices were ranked in the order of the total number of points received. Choices that received the same number of points (tie) were listed in random order.

Those questions that required the participants to give a yes or no answer were scored according to the total number of yes or no responses made.

All respondents had to answer the same questions, regardless of gender. The ARQ contained thirty-five questions, however, only twenty-seven questions were found to be useful for this project. The relevant questions, responses and comments of the sample group were incorporated into the text.

Appendix C

Demographic Information

The ARQ was administered to hundreds of single African-American adults, the majority of whom were students at Chicago State University (CSU), Chicago, Illinois. Approximately 65% of CSU students reside within a six-mile radius of the campus. A majority of CSU's students are nontraditional students who attend school while holding full-time jobs and/or raising families. Over two-thirds are female and 85% are African-Americans.

The detailed demographic breakdown of the resulting sample group is as follows:

Single African American Women

Age Group:	22-28	29-36	37-43	Totals
Number:	74	40	32	1 46
Marital Status:				
Single	70	30	17	1 17
Separated	2	3	2	7
Divorced	2	7	12	21
Widowed	0	0	1	1
Education:				
High school	5	4	3	12
Undergraduate	67	25	20	1 12
Bachelor	1	11	6	18
Masters	1	0	3	4
Doctorate	0	0	0	0

Single African American Women (Contd.)

Age Group:	22-28	29-36	37-43	Totals
Annual Income (Thousands)				
0 - 10	51	17	10	78
11 - 20	17	13	10	40
21 - 30	5	7	6	18
31 - 40	1	2	4	7
41 - 50	0	1	2	3
51 and above	0	0	0	0
Religious Background:				
Catholic	12	4	4	20
Christian	8	6	3	17
Baptist	36	16	15	67
Methodist	4	1	2	7
Pentecostal	1	1	1	3
Muslim	1	0	0	1
Other	12	12	7	31

Single African American Men

Age Group:	22-28	29-36	37-43	Totals
Number:	34	30	30	94
Marital Status:				
Single	31	22	21	74
Separated	2	2	3	7
Divorced	1	6	6	13
Widowed	0	0	0	0

Single African American Men (Contd.)

Age Group:	22-28	29-36	37-43	Totals
Education:				
High school	4	5	5	14
Undergraduate	26	16	7	49
Bachelor	4	7	13	24
Masters	0	2	4	6
Doctorate	0	0	1	1
Annual Income (Thousands):				
0 - 10	13	5	7	25
11 - 20	13	3	4	20
21 - 30	7	14	8	29
31 - 40	1	7	4	12
41 - 50	0	0	4	4
51 and above	0	1	3	4
Religious Background:				
Catholic	1	5	3	9
Christian	1	1	2	4
Baptist	18	13	12	43
Methodist	2	1	3	6
Pentecostal	0	1	0	1
Muslim	0	1	1	2
Other	12	8	9	29

References

Adamore, Raymond C. (1991). Adamore's Relationship Questionnaire, Unpublished work

Ali, Shahrazad (1989). *The Blackman's Guide to Understanding the Blackwoman*, Philadelphia, Pa., Civilized Publications

Ali, Shahrazad (1990). *The Blackwoman's Guide to Understanding the Blackman*, Philadelphia, Pa., Civilized Publications

Beauvior, Simone de (*1974*). *The Second Sex*, (H.M. Parshley, Trans/Ed.), New York, Vintage Books

Chapman, Audrey B. (1986). *Man Sharing: Dilemma or Choice*, New York, Kayode Publications Ltd.

Clancy, Jo (1996). *Anger and Addiction: Breaking the Relapse Cycle*, Madison, Connecticut, Psychosocial Press

Davis, Larry E. (1998). *Black and Single: Meeting and Choosing a Partner Who's Right for You*, New York, The Ballantine Publishing Group

Egwuonwu, Ani Dike (1986). *Marriage Problems in Africa*, New York, Continental Services

Ellis, Albert & Harper, Robert A. (1975). *A New Guide to Rational Living*, Hollywood, CA, Wilshire Book Company

Ellis, Albert (1996). *Better, Deeper And More Enduring Brief Therapy: The Rational Emotive Therapy Approach*, New York, BRUNNER/MAZEL Publishers

Gould, Roger (1975). *Adult Life Stages: Growth Towards Self-Tolerance*, Psychology Today, Vol. 8, No. 9, 74-78

Grant, Gwendolyn Goldsby (1995). *The Best Kind of Loving: A Black Woman's Guide to Finding Intimacy*, New York, HarperCollins Publishers, Inc.

Latif, Sultan A. & Latif, Naimah (1994). *Slavery: The African American Psychic Trauma*, Chicago, Illinois, Latif Communications Group, Inc.

Madhubuti, Haki R. (1990). *Black Men: Obsolete, Single, Dangerous?*, Chicago, Illinois, Third World Press

McMillan, Terry (1989). *Disappearing Acts*, New York, Viking

McMillan, Terry (1992). *Waiting to Exhale*, New York, Viking

Medol, Jerry (1986). The Gift of Anger, Unpublished work

Millner, Denene (1997). *The Sistahs' Rules: Secrets for Meeting, Getting, and Keeping a Good Black Man,* New York, William Morrow and Company, Inc.

Millner, Denene and Chiles, Nick (1999). *What Brothers Think, What Sistahs Know: The Real Deal on Love and Relationships,* New York, William Morrow and Company, Inc.

Millner, Denene and Chiles, Nick (2000). *What Brothers Think, What Sistahs Know About Sex*, New York, William Morrow and Company, Inc.

References

Russell, Kathy, Wilson, Midge & Hall, Ronald (1992). *The Color Complex: The Politics of Skin Color Among African Americans* New York, Random House, Inc.

Ryan, Christopher and Cacila Jetha' (2010), *Sex At Dawn*, New York, HarperCollins Publishers

Ury, William L. (1999,2000). *The Third Side: Why We Fight and How We Can Stop*, New York, Penguin Books

Walker, Lenore E. (1979). *The Battered Woman,* New York, HarperPerennial

Willis, Jay Thomas (1990). *Implications for Effective Psychotherapy with African-American Families and Individuals*, Matteson, Illinois, Genesis Publications

Yankura, Joseph & Dryden, Windy (1997). Using REBT with common psychological problems: A therapist's casebook. In Terjesen, Mark D., DiGiuseppe, Raymond & Naidich, Jennifer (Eds) *REBT for Anger and Hostility,* (pp. 158-196), New York, Springer Publishing Company